PLANET STEWARD

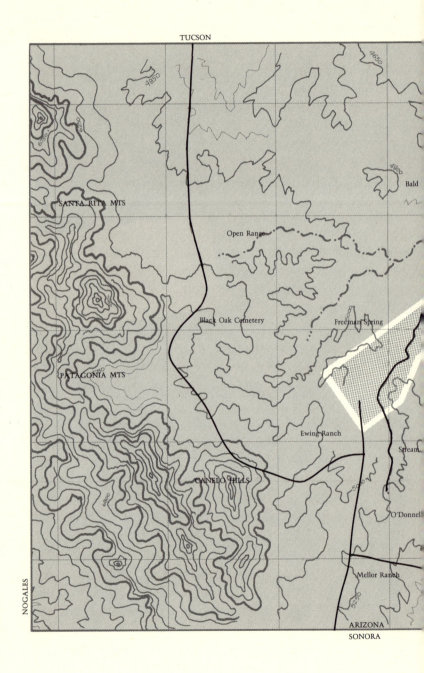

TUCSON

4850

4650

4900

Bald

SANTA RITA MTS

Open Range

Black Oak Cemetery

Freeman Spring

PATAGONIA MTS

Ewing Ranch

Stream

CANELO HILLS

O'Donnell

NOGALES

Mellor Ranch

ARIZONA

SONORA

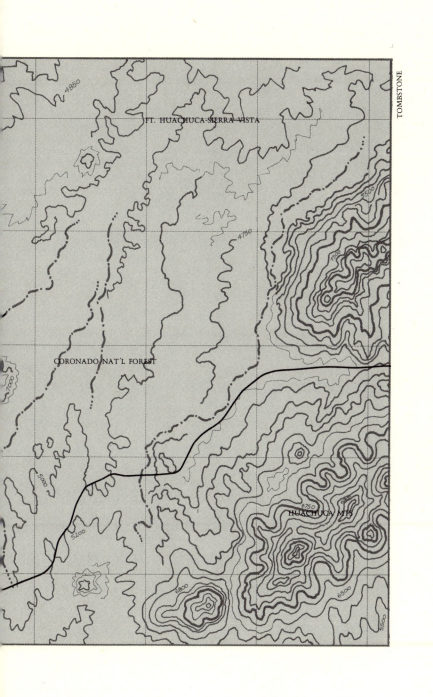

FT. HUACHUCA-SIERRA VISTA

CORONADO NAT'L FOREST

HUACHUCA MTS

TOMBSTONE

PLANET STEWARD
Journal of a Wildlife Sanctuary

Stephen Levine

Illustrated by Armando Busick

 UNITY PRESS ⁀ *SANTA CRUZ*

PUBLISHED JUNE 1974 BY
UNITY PRESS, BOX 1037, SANTA CRUZ, CALIFORNIA 95061
SECOND PRINTING 1975

Grateful acknowledgement is made to the
following for permission to use materials:
BLACK ELK SPEAKS © 1932, '59, '61 John Neihardt
ARIZONA HIGHWAYS © 1969 for research
by James Serven on history of horses
in the Southwest.
Carol Osmond Brown, ARIZONA HIGHWAYS © 1969
ARIZONA WILDLIFE VIEWS © 1969 for quotations
used in August fence episode.

LIBRARY OF CONGRESS CATALOGING IN PUBLICATION DATA
LEVINE, STEPHEN
    PLANET STEWARD
        1. CANELO HILLS CIENEGA, ARIZ.   2. WILDLIFE
CONSERVATION—ARIZONA I. TITLE
    QH76.5.A6L48   333.9'5'0979179   73-76671
            ISBN 0-913300-30-6
            ISBN 0-913300-32-2 (PBK)

Designed by
ED PENNIMAN & CRAIG CAUGHLAN

PRINTED IN THE UNITED STATES OF AMERICA

DEDICATED TO

Patricia who shared so much for so long

And to those who in the four years completion have become part of the work: Nick Harvey, Beth Cooper, Raymond Davis, Armando Busick, Mark Lawshe, Richard Felger, Craig Caughlan, Betsy Graceful and Sweet Maida. Too, I wish to thank the editors of the various publications in which portions of this book first appeared: *Zietetic Press Monograph Series, The Sun, Place, Omen, New York Quarterly, Maitreya, Kyoi, Gayatri Newsletter* and *Astral Projection.*

INTRODUCTION

In 1969 I offered Stephen Levine the job of caretaker for a piece of land in southern Arizona, a nature preserve known as the Canelo Hills Cienega. The land was chosen to be saved in as undisturbed a state as possible because it is one of the last intact examples of what much of this part of the country was once like, and because of the richness and diversity of life-forms that depend on it as an oasis: a place where the primordial and delicate chains of life have never been broken. Stephen Levine was chosen to watch over this precious natural area because of his capacity for responsible land stewardship and because of his poet's awareness. I felt he would have the ability to observe and appreciate the complexity, power and beauty of this place, and to communicate this awareness to others.

For over ten years as Western Regional Director of the Nature Conservancy and now President of the Trust for Public Land I have witnessed unforgettable human-land relationships. Land is rarely saved, in fact, unless a strong human force is involved. And this necessary force, as I have eventually come to realize, is an intangible human awareness, an awareness which must be uncovered and nurtured in all of us. Intangible as it is in its beginnings its harvest is of equal value to wheat or gold. It is difficult to grasp the essence of this awareness—as difficult as trying to capture the fragrance of a rose by filling a jar with the surrounding air. Yet it is possible. Thoreau and Aldo Leopold succeeded. And their awareness became a force that is changing people's lives.

So I have tried to channel some contemporary man-land experiences into tangible form by aiding others who might, through literature, photographs or statements of belief, provide a means of sharing their vision. Sending artists to be caretakers of land is frustrating if only because they don't always conform to the traditional 'business management requirements'. But although these efforts often fell short, they have been successful enough to make me keep trying. This time, a poet has delivered a dream, and *Planet Steward* is a rich reward for the effort.

The poetry of Stephen's book incorporates philosophy, courage and beauty into a needed new planet awareness. It is another step toward helping man to realize that he is part of the living world, but that man is wrong in trying to be omnipotent in it. Stephen's love of life and his openness to all parts of it—from ant hill to cosmos—make his experience worthy of being shared. City dwellers who may never be able to work or live in the way the Levines did can perhaps better appreciate what is involved in such a commitment.

And now, maybe for the first time, we have a book which park and land management students and professionals can read, which can describe the meaning of an 'aesthetic' view. Non-consumptive use of land—not taking home a trophy—as occurs with poets, artists, photographers and hikers—is difficult to describe in academic terms.

This book, the result of a peaceful harvest at the

Canelo Hills Sanctuary, is an example of non-consumptive use of the land: human use of delicate landscapes without damaging them. The importance of non-consumptive land use has both a psychic and economic feasibility. From this concept develops a 'new tourism' supporting many while allowing others to experience unspoiled natural areas. Too, of great importance is the value that natural areas have for the maintenance of natural gene pools which have often been called upon by the agriculture industry to maintain endangered crops. An example being the massive blight on grapes in the Thirties which threatened to devastate the grape and wine industry. Had it not been for the availability of wild native American grape root stocks, which have now come to be used throughout the world, the industry would have been ruined. Other examples of the economic feasibility of maintaining natural areas is evidenced in the return of agricultural hybridizers to native wild specimens for the revitalization of threatened crops. Land is not wasted which is preserved, rather, it is 'banked' for future use.

The psychic and spiritual values of protected natural areas are brought to many through photographs and writings, and the sense of peace experienced by visitors. Such experiences are important rewards since they can become lifelong cherished memories.

All this, of course, on a non-consumptive basis can be repeated a thousand times without disrupting the land.

Among the many lessons in his book, one of the most valuable is in Stephen's positive handling of technology to repair the devastation caused by previous unplanned acts of man, his use of 'planet plumbing', in this case the building of a dam to save the cienega from erosion. I have never seen such a sensitive statement regarding the positive use of technology before. And yet that must be a central theme for our future planetary survival.

A word might well be said for those people who made it possible for the Canelo Hills Cienega to be preserved. The generosity of Mrs Cordelia Scaife May allowed the Nature Conservancy to make the original purchase. The members of the Canelo Hills Project Committee including Claire Ellinwood, Mrs R. B. Porter, the Serats, Greenleafs, Steeles, Duffields and others have dedicated many years of hard work and perseverance to the acquisition and protection of land. Their efforts continue, and they are now raising funds to pay for an addition to the Preserve—an adjacent piece of land which includes the headwaters of O'Donnell Creek—an area of vital importance to the integrity of the entire cienega. The Committee's ability to work steadily and skillfully in the traditional world of business is what allowed the Levines' experience in this unspoiled natural environment. And Stephen gives much in return. Those of us with a sense of business may be able to feel in our bones that a piece of land is worth preserving. It is the poet who articulates why.

The Levines' experience at Canelo Hills was thoroughly successful. They excelled not only in the caretaking role, but also in a prophetic and artistic role, which is what makes this book so important. Certainly their experience justifies efforts to find others, whether bank presidents or poets, who can pursue land stewardship. Each experience, and the sharing of it, brings us a step closer to a loving relationship between man and the land.

A whole generation is changing, seeking a new and better awareness, and in many cases returning to the land. An older generation can better appreciate those changes by reading this book. For all of us are changing. Be it energy shortages or increasing automation, many unforeseen influences will affect everyone's lifestyle in some way in the years ahead.

A person's age or style of life should have little effect on his attitude toward land. Everyone needs to share the 'planet steward' approach, whether he is concerned with a flower, a field or a nation, and Stephen has brought us closer to that realization.

I once asked Stephen how he came to be so interested in land. He told me that many of the places he played in as a child have been covered with concrete. The woods he remembers with creeks, birds and rabbits, all 'developed'. It is hard to go home with all the cement there. But in this book Stephen makes a classic philosophical breakthrough. He does so by demonstrating the universality of beauty. We have lost much, but viewed on a planetary scale, much still remains. So we can go home, as the entire planet is our household.

HUEY JOHNSON
San Francisco
March 15, 1974

"IT is the story of all life that is holy and is good to tell, and of us two-leggeds sharing in it with the four-leggeds and the wings of the air and all green things; for these are children of one mother and their father is one Spirit."

"This is my prayer; hear me! The voice I have sent is weak, yet with earnestness I have sent it. Hear me!"

Black Elk Speaks

A wildlife sanctuary is a state of mind, an attitude, protecting more than just the acreage it encompasses, exposing all to an alternative relationship with the land. A steward according to twentieth-century Webster is a ward or keeper entrusted with the management of the estate of another. This is a keeping of the household accounts, a journal of a year tending and tended by a wildlife sanctuary, a ledger of species and states of mind.

PRELUDE TO SANCTUARY

In the bathtub of our Sausalito home, dreaming through a Strout catalog of country real estate with nothing but warm water in my pocket, Patricia enters the room and hands me the phone—it is divine providence on the line. My knees rising like mountains from the lagoon in which I float to hear from an old friend the possibility that we might apply as caretakers for a wildlife sanctuary.

It is Allen Cohen, my co-editor for two years on the *San Francisco Oracle*, calling from Table Mountain Ranch in northern California, telling me he has heard that the Nature Conservancy, the national conservation group whose purpose is to acquire and preserve unique ecological niches, may have a position for a caretaker on one of its more than four hundred sanctuaries. Knowing that we were looking for a place on the land where we could pursue our vision quest he has called to offer this alternative.

A phone call to the Nature Conservancy office in San Francisco introduces us to the extraordinary Huey Johnson, Western Regional Director of the Conservancy, who invites us down for a chat. After seeing some of my writing and listening quietly to our expectations he tells us of the most treasured of the sanctuaries which he has jurisdiction over, an oasis marsh in the rolling desert prairie hills of O'Donnell Basin in southern Arizona just a dozen miles above the Mexican border.

17

Patricia and I return home excited with the possibility of the sanctuary offered. And so a week later we meet again with Huey Johnson to commit ourselves to a year caretaking the sanctuary: a year in which to find our original face reflected in the wilderness. For the Navahos three days on the mountain during the rites of passage allowed the adolescent to become an adult, returning to the tribe with his vision, knowing the path he must follow. Born of the New Mechanical Ice Age where adolescence often lasts a lifetime, we dedicate ourselves to a year to come to our senses, to return to seeing. To know the life we must lead.

And Huey Johnson, trusting his own vision enough to trust ours, hires us as caretakers to learn the work and play of planet stewardship, a twentieth century counterpart to the American Indians' wholistic attitude toward nature, his spiritual art.

We agree to leave for the sanctuary in five weeks, after Puff has whelped her puppies and life may safely continue its migration. Before leaving we drive north to say goodbye to our friends at Table Mountain, leaving them our old Chevy panel truck for their communal use. In generous return, knowing our need for a conestoga wagon for the trek to our new homestead they offer us the hull of an old Volkswagen bus, empty-engined for two years in the field, used as a playhouse by the children whose beautiful scribblings from the collective unconscious adorn the inside paneling. And as divine providence would have it, while visiting friends in nearby Albion someone by chance asks, "You wouldn't happen to need this Volkswagen engine I have sitting in my garage, would you?" The next

18

day we insert the engine into the Volksbus and our covered wagon is appointed for the journey to sanc-tuary.

JUNE

THE OLD HAND-PAINTED VOLKS coveredwagon, christened 'Divine Providence' and stuffed with life and life's miscellany. The dogs, a dozen boxes of pots and pans, a couple of oriental rugs, the friendly books and records, the Mexican typewriter, a few worn tools and the human family, headed a thousand miles to sanctuary. Seeking our niche like some evolutionary creature thrown from the sea onto a deserted beach, we leave the primordial ooze of the city for a cleaner higher world.

The potlatch of moving: an overflow of goods left behind, absorbed by a dozen friends come to wish us well. Their pickup trucks and back seats piled high with the residue of our years of householding.

Mama dog and her two pups scuttling through the long-legged stool and over the typewriter into her nest by the rear window, then up for a potato chip and back again. The old engine slightly herniated by the load. Heading down the Imperial Valley through summer crops, slow as a pregnant hippo. Lettuce like a green glacier stretched across the wide valley, eating the alkaline earth, strafed with insectdeath, birdless. Fresno a bingo card stapled neon along the highway. Bakersfield at the end of the freeway slide, and up the mountain at fifteen miles an hour cresting past dying ponderosa pine, entering the valley of Los Angeles, yellow smog-slick creeping like lava into every crevice, lichen dry

as beached seaweed. Life leaking from those giant pon-
derosas, deprived of sun and air by the smoky yellow
cat of industry, mouse on catclaw, unable to escape,
terminal. And motel plastic, magic to the touch, in
dead sleep of roaddazed exhaustion, five hundred miles
down and sore all over. But in the days when we went
a thousand miles by horse or ox-drawn covered wagon,
the first day hardly took us beyond the ranches that
skirted St. Joseph. Fifteen miles was a good day. And
you walked most of the way, keeping those heedless
cattle to the fore. Dreaming.

The food available while on the road is toxic . . .
hamburgers and malts, artificial bread and frosty
freezes, making me think we should be like the tiny
ruby-throated hummingbirds who fly five hundred
miles nonstop across the Gulf of Mexico without eating, that a migration and a fast seem good together.
But instead we eat steak for protein and drive all night
across the flat white desert of lowland California, approaching Arizona at a hundred degrees Fahrenheit,
two in the morning, passing through the eye of Needles,
California, onto Indian Arizona.

And through the myth-riddled mountains, wary of
the other wagons on the trail, trying to keep on our
side of the line, bleary eyed, just a few hundred miles
to go; no buckets or sinks abandoned on the trail, no
steer skulls, no fever, all the children still alive. A jug
of cold water on the floorboards beside us, the hostiles
never met, a safe journey toward homestead, past road
signs of the magic mantra of the Southwest: Open
Range. Twentieth century America, sanctuary.

June 25   *A Papago hammerstone in the mouth*
of mama dog. First archeological find;
first welcome from the planet.

We have landed. Four days on the road has led us
to the nonexistent township of Canelo Hills, Arizona:
a sign swaying above two abandoned gas pumps rusting
a few miles down the dusty road.

Arrived at sanctuary, sensing we have found our
place at last, this migration more than a thousand
miles, beginning at the womb continuing on to this
moment. And perhaps Thomas Wolfe was wrong and
indeed we can go home again, home to the planet.

We are greeted by two of the local Nature Conservancy Committee, a geologist and an ornithologist who
welcome us to our new home and spend a few hours
introducing us to sanctuary. The principles of our position are once more outlined. To protect the sanctuary
from hunters, collectors and those who would litter
the wilderness. To chronicle nature measuring rainfall
and temperature change. To be on fire watch. To guide
those who visit, making sure no one falls in a gopher
hole or trips headlong into an open arroyo. And finally
our job is to simply be a human presence in tune with
the land, for which the Committee can offer us no
guidelines, as the experiment is our own. To tend the
land, to tend in the sense of attention, to bring our consciousness to the healing processes through which the
land might pass given the appropriate consideration,
our duty is to the planet itself, to watch and learn and
become stewards initiated by the life all about us.

Patricia, yearling Tara and I allowing nerve ends to uncoil from the ardors of migration. Divine Providence weary in the wide green shade of a Mexican blue oak. Slowly unpacking what we need as we need it, nesting.

June 26   *Lightning mesmerizing the sky*
                             from charcoal black cloud caves.

Cottonwoods sink enormous roots to drink from the stream; their green billowy oceanic tops can be seen waving miles away as one approaches the sanctuary, a green geyser above the rusting oak-grassland hills.

Eighty year old apple trees, planted by the frontiersman buried beneath the front porch, droop with hundreds of small green apples. Untouched for years, uncultivated. Pruned by the gusty southeastern wind.

Eight hundred feet from the house, across the thick green cienega, the stream cathedrals a world of riparian life. Now billions of years after that first shock of life the planet takes on ten thousand forms to produce the motions and creatures which we meet. Just by approaching the stream the meditation is begun.

Everywhere there are birds which have immigrated as we and the original homesteader have, in flight across the red shale and desert brownness, spying in the distance the green oval of this remarkable oasis. Their calls fill the air. In morning the doves claim domain as the owls and nighthawks preen for sleep.

June 27   *Brittle grass harps in the wind.*

Although this is the dryest year in the past seventeen, the marsh is yet thick and full of life. At night gymnast fireflies dance above sedge and spikebrush. All about us the cattlemen seek water. The Papago Indians have already lost a thousand head of the tribal herd. We too have our consciousness centered on water: the old well is polluted, *E. coli* bacilli, a fallen rat's nest half-sunk at the bottom.

We acclimate to this new human and desert community. At first the changes in magnetics, altitude, climate and sunfire ratio create a physical feedback: Tara runs a 102° temperature for two days, her fever breaking late the third day in chuckles and a new vitality; Patricia rising out of an energy drain about the same time. Now we are feeling better than ever, becoming each day more another animal on the land.

June 28   *History beneath the fingernails.*

The Mexican Figaroa family and I labor to clear fallen adobe bricks from the weather-torn southeastern corner of the eighty year old house. Angelo, the father, and his two teenage sons work at ease in the intense desert sun. They rest when they are tired, eat when they are hungry.

Installing the new propane gas tank, water heater, stove, toilets and shower; civilizing the house.

26

June 29

The house has not been lived in by humans for over seven years, and we have many friends of different species overlooking our cleaning and repair operations. Spiders own the corners, their carcass-hung webs doming each room. Deer mice scudding between the walls. And as I am writing now, above my head somewhere between the ceiling and the roof there is a creature, probably a pack rat, perhaps attracted by the sounds of the typewriter and the vibration of the writing. When I move across the room he scampers audibly but invisibly overhead, stopping where I stop, sitting or circling a bit, then running back across the room with me. I knock on the ceiling and he does a greeting dance; he does not seem afraid, nor do I. Perhaps one day we will meet with a start and become friends. Until then we are a mysterious element in each other's life. Could he be Dostoyevsky in a new life, living out his underground man syndrome, occupying that same habitat? Until we are better met I shall henceforth refer to him as Fyodor.

June 30   Demagnetization.

Moving from one area of the planet to another, one undergoes a multitude of subtle variations. Having changed positions within the magnetic field of the planet the psyche seems to constellate in slightly different manners. It is noticeable particularly in the emotional body. The base energies, those which support and transmit life, seem the most affected: the way food moves through the hidden canals of the intestines, the sexual impetus, the appetite, the beating of the heart, the dry presence of the throat and involuntary swallowing. Speech slows, the head empties, the mind associates rather than 'thinks'. The involuntary actions of the body take the fore. Mind spins like a pointer in a compass attempting to find its way to magnetic north.

Having come from the sea-level hem of the Pacific Ocean we find the air here more rarefied than we are used to: altitude 5,200 feet, one mile high in the blue southwestern atmosphere. It is not difficult to see how the Navaho may be the Tibetan's counterpart in this hemisphere, right down to the skull structure, descent of the brow and outcropping cheekbones, and the ornamentation of silver and turquoise shared. Grand Canyon the planet's yoni, Everest the lingam. Here the element is fire, there it is ice.

In Tibet one can ride across an open plain with the skin on the back of the arms blistering from the direct rays of the sun while the feet, in shadow beneath the belly of the horse, freeze and suffer frostbite. Here one might blister during the day and be frozen by night.

In the great green forests of mammalian California from which we have just come the competition is for fire, the sun; water is plentiful, the hillsides covered with a golden pelt of European grasses. But here in the reptilian Southwest fire is the constant, which creates in its turn a life competition for water, segmented choya and fish-claw ocatillo like scales on earth python. The polarities swung full cycle.

JULY

July 1
An overview of sanctuary.
Each species a facet of the gem.

THE FAT SUMMER SUN breaks over purple rim of the Huachuca Mountains flooding the wide basin with first morning gold, though the steadily brightening sky has already begun day for a hundred species. The direct rays of the sun wake a thousand insects warming to the day, mobile once again. The first shaft of light lifts a golden eagle from her ledge in search of rabbit and rodent. Her two eaglet chicks, big as rabbits themselves, wait noisily for breakfast's return. Father circles in the sun as heat rebounds from the oak-savannah grassland of the Coronado National Forest which surrounds the sanctuary beginning ten miles to the east, three thousand feet below the burning peaks of the sunrise Huachucas. Birds rise from agavi fortresses in the high Sonoran desert grasslands, slaloming through Spanish bayonet and serrated yuccas. A shiny black stag-horn beetle edges through a wiry clump of long thin bear grass waving like a kinetic sculpture in the warming breeze. A dozen forms of cactus march imperceptibly uphill to the oaks' retreat. The land drying, a bit more desert each year, making greater room for rainbow, hedgehog and prickly pear cactus, and along the drier areas the disheveled sentry of an occasional cholla. Etched through these rolling grassland hills, like the palm of an ancient warrior, are the shadowy dry ravines dominated by magical jimson weed and the quarter-size hoofprints of javelina. Coyote tracks trace the rim, seeking the darting rodents of the lower ground.

The sun filters down the Huachucas' western slope through grasses growing in the empty trails of bighorn sheep, long since gone from the purple rock and red shale of the mountainside. Another casualty of this century, the Mexican brown grizzly, equally absent. A lone rambling black bear reminds the sawtoothed mountains of what has been lost since man widened the animal paths.

Sunfire crosses the rolling and dipping metropolis of hills, passing through a swale of brush-covered quail, touching O'Donnell Canyon where blooms sanctuary. Sporadically, solitary Arizona white oaks rise above the sacaton-peaked grasslands, outposts to the miniature forests, seemingly shrunk by the desert sun, of twisted Emory and Mexican blue oak descending toward the stream and sanctuary. The turkey vulture and the red-tailed hawk wait in the tallest trees above the creek to rise on high swirling thermal currents to view their domain from a thousand feet up in the southwestern blue. Beside the stream under squaw bush a tiny ground dove shrugs the night from soft feathers, while in the air a mourning dove and a whitewing coo and flutter to the rising of the sun. From the Arizona walnuts which shade the sanctuary's stream comes the heavy flutter of band-tailed pigeons. The sun has already dried the grassland where once great communities of prairie dogs and their companions, the burrowing owl and the black-footed ferret, have long since departed, not even pitting the worn earth with their history. Their fertile remains have nourished the hun-

33

gry desert, raising flower, herb, shrub, and tree, wreaths for their sad demise. Gray fox moves through the morning silent as a falling acorn. In the dense Emory oak groves an Arizona woodpecker raps his morning calculation of the cosmos to a coatimundi rummaging for insects under the gray and brown stones on the hillside. Bits of fossil coral have worked their way up through the warming soil to jewel the desert grassland, where great herds of pronghorn antelope once gathered. The wild turkey and the pronghorn decimated by the Forty-niners who took the southern passage up through Mexico, bypassing the Rockies like those first Spaniards on their way to the fabled cities of gold. Gray wolf eluding history crouches in his den.

The night song of the mockingbird becomes day as nighthawk and poorwill descend. A restless flycatcher muttering as a flock of sparrows rain into the insect-filled grama grass unnoticed by a browsing white-tailed deer. Butterflies rise as fireflies disappear. The day is officially begun, seven a.m., and the birds have been up for hours.

A golden light overflows O'Donnell Canyon, watershed for the sixty square mile basin where an underground stream is forced to the surface to make this area unique: the flowing spine of the sixty acre long rectangle of sanctuary; the only permanent water at this altitude for one hundred forty miles east to New Mexico or forty miles west to Patagonia, an emerald oasis shared by one hundred twenty species of birds and hundreds of mammals and reptiles.

The sun entering sanctuary ignites the tips of tall cottonwoods above the stream, roost of Cooper's and

34

red-tail, blue heron and goshawk. Next the Goodding willow begins to warm, sheltering the owls heard each evening in their dark forays after scuffling gophers or unwary skunks. Below the porcupine's cottonwood and the owl's willow are the Arizona walnut and the ash, nesting places for scores of birds. From the ground beneath this multilevel streamside community rise the grasses, flowers, and herbaceous plants. Shrubs, squaw bush, white and yellow currants flick with warblers, grosbeaks and hummingbirds. Scarlet lobelia and spring violets unsuccessfully cross-pollinate with yellow monkey flowers to gem the moss carpet that banks the stream. Everywhere the acrobat woodpeckers: acorn woodpeckers glide from cottonwoods into an oak tangle, red-shafted flickers rise and drop like waves, white patches flashing above the grassland, the gila woodpecker bobbing for an apple at the end of a branch, the ladderback sipping from the spinal fluids of the stream, center of all life at sanctuary. Gazing down on the swirling bird-dance from the tops of a cottonwood a sluggish porcupine grunts as the sun rinses night from his quills. Hawks peer to grassland seeking morning sustenance as owls roost for a long sleep.

Tree frog, turtle, and leopard frog take their turn in the early morning ballet on the moist moss banks reflected in the dark currents of the stream. Their reflection pierced by the native fish who find this stream a last refuge: the dace, gila and the endangered sucker *Catostomus*, who now exists perhaps nowhere else but in these few miles of stream. Each finding his piscean vector as distinct as the flight patterns of birds, zigzagging from duckweed to cress beneath the strafing shadow of a scarlet biplaned dragonfly. These are the waters of sanctuary, risen above ground level a few miles south of the fence, to disappear once again underground a mile to the north.

The sun arcs above the hundred foot tall cottonwoods, gilding the grassy border where eighty years ago frontiersman Whitehill planted quince and apple and four Parthenon-straight pecan trees separating the riparian community from the wet meadow, the marshy cienega. The ground soaked just beneath its surface, a boggy home for sedge, abundant buttercups, curious blue-eyed grass, rare primrose, blue violet, and a sea of wildflowers, cienega fire to jewel the summer. Like tresses along either side of the cienega a rare orchid, *Spiranthes graminea*, sighted for the first time in thirty years, whose tiny white trumpets swirl toward the sun. The basic cienega community dominated by rushes and spikebrush, tules and flowering herbaceous plants so conspicuous in spring and early summer. The vermilion flycatcher sings his morning song as he glides above the green eye of the cienega from apple to oak seeking a mate with his crimson display of ardor and acrobatics. Below in the morning's first shadow a rabbit huddles, his head between his shoulders, attempting invisibility in the shadow of a swooping prairie falcon, his heart resonating with the piercing shriek of a cotton rat captured in the steel gray coils of a gopher snake a few yards away. Like the prairie falcon the cienega itself is an endangered species, a geological relic from a time when the water tables were higher and the land not so overgrazed or eroded. The cienega, like the swamp from which we sprang, is a harsh and

36

tuneful cradle.

The sun progresses to the swamp trill of a red-winged blackbird in the marsh household grown up about the two springs that overflow into the cienega beyond the willow border. Tules and cattails rise in profusion from the dark standing water. In cattails' shadow the lilting song sparrow and the self-conscious rail find their way, heeding an inquisitive raccoon who scratches the dark mud and sniffs the clear air. Again the red-wing yodels from atop a fat cattail, heraldic squire of the marsh showing off to his well-nested children shaded by a giant mulberry, carpeted in cress.

And now the direct rays of the sun are everywhere, reaching the habitat of man beyond the two hundred foot strip of grassland which now returns to its natural succession after being disturbed by years of farming and overgrazing vehicles parked beside the dirt road. Pioneer plants take hold as best they can: alligator-barked juniper, prickly poppy, mallow and evening primrose, the disruption of natural order having allowed other species to enter like the flourishing horse-high Johnson grass, a European immigrant arriving in the late 1880s, its seeds brought in on the coats of old world livestock just before the massive overgrazing.

Across the road man's dominion rises as an eighty year old adobe homestead fortress, our two and half foot thick walled home—home too for mice from the grassy fields, a large gray rock squirrel under the eaves, a mountain king snake departing from the abandoned fireplace upon our arrival. Through the saguaro rafters of the first floor can be seen the webs, eggs and migrations of the insect people. An alligator lizard high on the wall, the best indoor insecticide we know, frees our minds of centipede, black widow and triatoma. Though we are willing to share our home with most we discourage the presence of the rare rock rattler and black-tailed rattler encouraging them to join their harmless cousins the Sonoran whip snake, gopher, ring neck, and the several designs of garter whom we gently broom off the doorstep into the grasslands that swallow the house. A horned toad, orange and dusty, peers up from the corner of the porch to question his reptile place as a pigmy mouse scampers for protective shade away from Sir Rattler's diamond eyes.

Patricia, Tara and I release our two dogs for their morning romp, the night creatures having been allowed their free reign of the closely hunted moonlit woods and grassland. Diamond dew on the dogs' sleek coats reflects the sunrise in their city free lunging. The sun begins to soak the heavy house, woman and child munching toast on the porch, horses chomping oats in the corral, I brewing poetry at the typewriter.

Afternoon sun slides up the oak-grassland hillside toward the flattop mesa that rises behind the house. The surrounding oak savannah punctuated by the ever present summer flowers. The delicate white Sonora star lily shadows a dozen different flower fellows, the succulent pink chromorian momentarily eclipsed while the mandala-top rainbow cactus waits patiently for the shadow to pass, surrounded by a dense mat of al-most microscopic euphorbia petals.

And we are at the center of life, coming each day a bit closer to what we share with all that exists about us. A great variety of species come together in this same sanctuary roost. We are the northerly range for certain South American birds as well as the southerly range for various arctic and northern Canadian species. Out of Mexico for a while, the karakara warms himself on these grasslands while the gray hawk hunts overhead. The green kingfisher, squawking South American cousin of the common belted kingfisher who winters here from the north, takes up residence in sanctuary, accompanied by his southern companions the becard and trogan and the tropical kingbird, to roost side by side in early spring and late fall with the northern species who migrate to this broad overlapping range. From the evergreen forests of Canada the red crossbill and the evening grosbeak come to pluck seeds from the conifers while at home in thick dark evergreen forests snow covers their food supply. Escaping winter from the north come the goshawk, marsh hawk and rough-legged hawk. Summer approaches with the yellow grosbeak, the five-striped sparrow, and the thick-billed kingbird extending their range from the south with new changes in world climate.

The sun crosses the grassland hills which lead toward the Patagonia and Santa Rita Mountains, its flame-nest roost on our western horizon, passing over climax forests of pinion pine on the Canelo Hills where once roamed mammoths, mastodons, antlered giraffes, giant ground sloths, the native wild horse and camel and the great American lion, all extinct since the last Pleistocene ice age, probably wiped out by Paleolithic man's expert hunting guilds. Unafraid Pleistocene animals met man for the first time in an encounter the animals did not survive. Perhaps the very change in climate which allowed man to move into this virgin environment twelve thousand years ago made it difficult for these great mammals to continue. And still many ecological niches are unfilled: even another twelve thousand years will not be enough time to replace the species destroyed by ancient man in a time when America must have looked very much like Africa of the nineteenth century.

The sun passes history about a half mile west behind the mesa, dropping down to Freeman's Spring where the tracks of a mountain lion lead into the unseen imagined. The sun casts long pyramids from the base of a giant juniper as manzanita and mesquite throw spider shadows on the hard desert soil. Oak pierced by the last red rays of the sun. Tarantula and red ant, lizard and scorpion shadow the roots of flowing grama: ringtail and rabbit, roadrunner and rattler, glow as the sun sets into the incredible firesweep sky above the Santa Rita Mountains, volcano-purple clouds steaming with the setting sun, fire behind the camel's back. The mountains recall the molten solidification of the planet, reminded by the sun of what is left to be preserved, that all is sanctuary.

July 2   *A patchwork of moving shadows like a flock of migrating swans.*

The first pancake-thin clouds of the last few days have, today, swelled in the southeast into the great puffy dark-bottomed harbingers of the first much-needed summer rains, passing over with the wild, tumbling winds that rise out of the Huachucas and darken as all await that first life-fortifying downpour. But after the winds and the beginning sprinkles, nothing. Darkness broken through by sun and the continuous thunder that has shaken the sky all afternoon.

Patricia and I making love, attempting to bring on the life-giving rains the only way we know how. Greater thunder and the reappearance of raindrops on the half-open window just beside us. The dark canopy stretches to the mountains rising out of Mexico, our horizon forty miles to the south. As I type this page I am certain that my whole life has led me to this moment, that all my actions, all the writing, watching, listening, faltering, centering, mistakes and accidents have brought me to Now, have led to this moment, to the passing on of the wonder of this place.

July 3   *A day of birds and verse.*

The birds are wild with the wind today
their matings catapult from treetops
pinwheels merging in mid-air
furrows carved in the warm
southeastern breezes. Their
songs like prayers from an adjoining room.

Today we rebuild the rock wall in front of the adobe house, hot stones in steady hands, reshaping fallen remnants of the past, the present clear as earth beneath our fingernails.

Knowing that anything written
lacks the continuity
humming in my genes.

Perhaps the time has come for typing on a roll of paper instead of separate sheets. Just by changing paper the continuum is interrupted while a dozen creatures pass to hawk claw and are born again in the wild thicket by the spring, beneath the food-filled mulberry.

July 4   *Interdependence Day.*

The first summer rains have begun in stupendous nightly lightning storms and enormous thunderheads, initiated in short sprinkles, then an occasional gusty downpour. It is time to complete our plans for the earth retention dam across the stream. A dam seems the only way to preserve the cienega in the upcoming rains which will continue to cut back the stream's ten foot waterfall, carving the stream bottom down to bedrock, dropping the water table, draining ground waters, drying the cienega. Similarly thousands of identical streamside marshes have drained and eroded over the past hundred years since the overgrazing of the great cattle herds and the cutting of the deep-rooted streamside trees created the arroyos that now characterize the Southwest. If nothing is done to reinforce the soft soils of the streambed's waterfall, the cienega will be lost forever.

The rains restore some of what the new inhabitants, missionaries and frontiersmen, recorded up to the mid-nineteenth century as 'inexhaustible stands of grass' —since replaced by the low dry shrubs and cacti of an immense lowland desert. A change in thoughtform from the American Indian planet insight to the slaughter-minded erosions of the cattle barons, the land manifesting the change in consciousness of the beings living upon her.

July 5   *A promise of monsoons.*

During the days ninety to one hundred degree heat. All about is dry and gold-brown except for the cienega and stream which are green as Mendocino. Yet soon all the desert will be green as these cottonwoods, rich as the bottom of the sea. Billowy green trees wave in the mountain bred winds. From the north, hot desert breezes push toward the low pressure areas of the Gulf of Mexico, stirring up the summer monsoon which all await. How different from that overwhelmingly wet winter we experienced in California! And this, I am told, may be the only planet that wobbles on its axis.

Listening to Mozart, Beethoven and the Beatles, arms slightly extended, slowly whirling, a slow-motion dervish, another creature at home in its natural habitat: Tara sings downstairs to the tune of 'Life Goes On'.

The apple trees, quince, black walnuts, pears, Chinese dates and oaks are about to give their sweet fruits. We attend their permission to gather and partake of this gracious bounty. Their leaves spread forth like the Tarot, open to be read by the interested passer-by.

Already much has been met and learned. I discourse

with the turkey vulture and the bridled titmouse, the thousand-formed spider and the mud turtle, the javelina and the deer that come at sunset to the stream to drink and converse.

July 6   *Borrowing from the ancient humus.*

We have decided to plant a garden, to strike a bargain with the soil. We have encompassed our responsibility with a deer fence, cleared a ten-by-ten plot to be planted with vegetables, flowers and herbs which will feed us. In return we shall feed it, replacing at least as much as we have removed of the nutrients and moisture. The compost from our kitchen—the peels, pits, coffee grounds, left-over vegetables, shells of eggs— will be shredded, watered, and turned to decompose, mixed with the horses' manure and the sawdust from the splitting block, fed to the garden as the garden feeds us. The area about the garden a bit greener and lusher from the water and nutrients overflowing the hallowed plot. If it is ever possible to impart to our children a single life ethic it would be to clean up your messes— replace what you have taken, equalize the energy that has brought you to this moment. If you take from the soil, give to the soil. If the grass is chopped to the root and the soil deprived of its thousand year nutrient humus by incessant crops, a little bit less is left of the earth each year. Eventually you have a desert—a desert of the land and of the heart.

The Canelo Hills Sanctuary is not an 'open' sanctuary. Because of its delicate ecological balance only those involved in scientific research may visit by appointment, in keeping with the concepts of the Nature Conservancy: 'no picnicking, collecting or hunting.'

As a part of our job we are to act as guides to the sanctuary, though indeed what occurs is osmotic, passing on information gathered on previous walks. Many of the visitors to whom the Committee grants access are ornithologists who point out to us the flights and songs of various birds, entomologists who introduce us to shiny beetle life, paleobotanists who explain from fossil pollens the local ecosystem a million years ago, biochemists and geologists detailing soil structure and the microlife therein, historians recalling those who have walked upon this earth, archeologists telling us of those buried beneath it: each an expert in a facet of the whole, yet often so close to a personal specialty as to miss other aspects of the gem. We become the catalysts which combine the input of their knowledge to pass it on as though we too were experts, though indeed we are only the ciphers for a great mass of knowledge which we interrelate, living on the land away from the universities and microscopes of the scientists. Last week from the University of Arizona a graduate student in entomology came to study the altered feeding habits of a common horsefly which normally lives on the blood of large mammals but which has mutated into a nectar-sipping strain: Ferdinand of the horseflies. Today another visitor by appointment, an authority on the Yaqui Indians of northern Mexico. Her work for many years has been with the Yaqui culture and various personal relationships within that group. Arthritis kept her from leaving her automobile so we sat beneath the cottonwoods next to the waterfall cutback and spoke of the 'sciatica anima,' the 'flower body' of the Yaquis, the extrasensory presence within certain beings which makes them at one with what is about them, generally free of sickness, the best of the hunters and poets. Our job as custodian is one of great learning. The birds cut white paths in the wind.

July 9   *Black widow spider sat down beside her*
         so he stuck in his thumb
         and pulled out a gun
         and said 'what a transient creature am I.'

The meaning of the word 'survival' gains new momentum. Tara centers us on the harmonies and obstacles of our environment. That imagined scorpion of every parent's nightmares occasionally creeps about the corners of our vision. Each sentient being brings us closer to a harmony with the land while strengthening the mind in survival decisions: we try to be conscious of the divinity of each creature while acutely aware of our desire for Tara to survive. We put unwanted insects and the like gently outside on a torn-off matchbook cover or piece of paper; but at times when some threatening creature is out of reach, in a crevice or beneath the radiator, he may be injured in our at-

46

tempts to remove him. Though some prayer be said, this occasional taking of life gives us much thought. Yet the continuity of the miraculous life/death dance finds me bagging (burlap, that is) a porcupine couple on the mesa behind the house, on the Ewing ranch, so that Bud Ewing doesn't have to shoot them to protect his much-loved dogs—though porcupines are nocturnal and dogs should be kept in at night. Ewing agreed quite readily to my suggestion of moving rather than shooting them: he will find their home and notify me. I have spoken too with the local ranchers about not shooting that bear that some have seen and others have conjured. The cycle continues.

July 12

Only a few members of the local Nature Conservancy committee, to whom we are directly 'responsible', are agile and interested enough to hike with us through these marshes, outcroppings, meadows and streams. I begin to learn the ten thousand forms that have arisen from the One: names, shapes, properties, divinities, histories; how the soil came about, the different kinds of rock, the fossil pollens of plants that have preceded this voyager man by many eons; the calls of dozens of species; the tracks of carnivores, angels and wood nymphs, the dihedral sweep of the vulture, planet janitor; porcupine's nibblings as telltale signs; fox, badger, skunk, coyote; and heavy-handed, self-justifying man—the greatest of predators, the only saint.

The acorn woodpecker chips holes in the dying flesh of trees to implant a tasty acorn—a red-headed nun in the Library of Congress hoarding the past in empty knotholes, survival-sequestered in the stacks.

Each being here is the mother and sacrifice of every other. There is none that is not a perfect part of the whole. Each creature is indispensable, rising and falling in its time for the furtherance of every other creature. This is a place of breeding and feeding. The javelina grunts and chuckles in the full moon. The owl chants the night. Dove Orpheus coos up the sun. The flycatchers, titmice, grosbeaks, ravens, hawks, woodpeckers, eagles, vultures, sparrows, swifts, chats, mockingbirds, bluebirds and hummingbirds are strophe to the antistrophe of the crickets, beetles, fireflies, scarlet dragonflies, and the multiformed crawlings of moist unknowns. The turtle, algae on his shell, moves like a Zen garden across the duckweed. The native fish find dark cathedral in the winding stream. This is the planet brotherhood. And we rejoin the greater whole, becoming just another animal family on the land.

I write daily for at least an hour, do pranayama under cottonwoods, exchange early morning breath with Patricia. Tara tumbles into language like a frog into water. Dreams of Dharma melting pistols in the wide star-filled nights.

July 14

But it's not only alpha and omega. There is all the space between, the very noticeable effects on the emotions and the physical body (a time for neurons to unravel) that are involved in the demagnetization from the city. The nature of our energies is to be in a state of change. There are moments when thoughts race madly, tidal waves in the lake of mindstuff. Upon waking there is a daily reorientation to this desire for peace, the brotherhood of beings extending beyond the sanctity and disquietudes of man on into every creature. Though there seems a short-circuiting too, a kind of psychic feedback which lessens each day like electricity leaking from a highly charged object. We are like seeds planted too deeply within the soil, struggling in our germination toward the surface, toward the powerful source of life blazing above, approaching a state of grace, an attitude toward life which the land suggests and the city obstructs.

July 17   *Mockingbird chick found beneath apple tree, thrown from the nest by today's intense rainfall.*

Thunder over Mexico, a lightning-etched sky spectacular. The planet plumbing of the dam continues as nature's tides refill the once-drained pool, redrained again and troughed, filling with new rains once more, then drained again, generators buzzing like caged bees. A backhoe does the planet dentistry for the wingwalls, breaking down, then fixed and off again. Each worker selected for his experience and his sensitivity, each inspired by the planet-saving mission we are all on. Stumps removed from the waterfall's cutback pool, snakes and fish in the diminishing waters at the bottom of the pool removed by hand, sent downstream to regain their equilibrium within another pool, the roots of the giant cottonwoods carefully considered with each scoop of the backhoe digging the wingwalls near the family of trees by the cutback. A brown towhee's nest fills with eggs in the perfectly chaotic quince tree nearby. Work stopped each day before dusk so as not to scare away the many creatures who come to the stream. Life maintained sustaining this lush reality.

Happy birthday to me, thirty-two years old, and just beginning to find which way I'm facing.

July 18   *A day of introspective nostalgia.*

When I was a child, not knowing who I was, I felt like something at either end of a microscope. As an adolescent, taps on my heels, I thought I was the body. When I turned twenty-one, 'of age', I thought I was the mind, poetry as ambition. Passing thirty I tripped on heaven and became an angel. Now the spirit fills me and I don't exactly know what I am, nor do I fear not knowing.

July 20   *Eagle sets onto the Sea of Tranquility*
                           1:17 p.m.

Man is on the moon and today may be the changing of the Middle Way. Now that man sits on two celestial spheres, Luna and Terra, has the Aquarian Age begun?

It is said that this age begins with the one-pointed consciousness of the whole world on a singular happenstance. This concentration of world attention on the moon may be the Olympian torch which begins the new game. New archetypes breaking from the Collective Cortex into the flickering lights of the solar system. May there be no fences, no barbed wire, no flags, all Aquarian stronghold of the spirit! These first moonlanders returning enlightened, unwilling to assess their journey in scientific numerology, speaking instead of the green eye of God, this planet to which they return. These two men the forefathers of a new faith, a new sun worship that develops into the final monotheism: convergence! The separatist game is finished. God is not dead, only limitation. The Hopi chant of the Life Way sings in the chromosomes of future generations. An intuitive reception of a new world rising from each cell: a prayer contained in the last Piscean wheeze.

July 21

Ten pears from a kitchen basket found at the base of the stairs leading to the second floor where we sleep. Our dreams going out for a bite to eat—or are those the teethmarks of Dostoyevsky the rat?

July 22   *White rain brings yellow flowers from green grass.*

Last night during monsoon rains I met Fyodor on the

dark staircase at one a.m.—me with a flashlight, he with an apple. An adrenalin-surge acknowledgment of each other's reality. Friends soon, I suspect.

July 23   *The New Mechanical Ice Age, like that last cicada of autumn, by singing shall destroy itself.*

Planet plumbing continued. Concrete for one wing-wall poured yesterday, another to be dug today. What a ballet of machine and human energy on behalf of the planet! The machines of this technology might take us beyond the technology, much as reason takes us beyond reason itself. We are in a crucial time of game-change; we must elevate the game if we are to continue. Game: the lifedance. Nature: that out of which man has risen, to which he may, through lack of forethought, return, dissolve unnoticed, perhaps to be replaced at the summit of evolution by the porpoise or the ant. Poor social wolf never had a chance. Though man may be the most evolved species he may not be evolving as rapidly as other species, just ahead a furlong or two in the immense galaxy of evolution. The streets we paste to the earth; the buildings we poke into her and the power lines we spin across her will perhaps become irrelevant, a sloppy patchwork, a means of forcing nature to conform to our limitations. Future evolution may grace other creatures to adapt more intelligently to the requirements of the whole.

52

July 27   *Mail in the morning like seeing myself*
           in a history book.

"How does the green eye of God feel about your being there?": A letter from a friend. At first there may have been a bit of conjunctivitis, we being foreign matter bred of the cities. But as our demagnetization settles us more and we become stiller, things seem to come closer the continuum. At first we saw very little wildlife except for undifferentiated birds and a squirrel or two. Then into that second week, toting water because of the polluted well, we came more into the pupil of that greenness, seeing deer, porcupine, flickers and finches. Recognizing nightshade and prickly poppy, coming upon the nests of hummingbirds and towhees, introduced to blue-eyed grass by the thunder of the first summer rains. Waking each morning less scrambled than the day before. Finding present each day the necessary energies that bring this old house back to a livable and safe condition.

Tara sunned and glowing in first tuggings and steps. Quiet evenings cricketed and coyoted. Watching lightning walk across the peaks of the purple Huachucas, fire moving through air to earth accompanied by rain, the four elements unabstracted.

Sitting on the front porch playing a wooden flute to the melody of coincidence, passing from moment to moment, I become the Missing Link: watching tarantula walk slowly across the dirt road; understanding what survival means from more centers than my own.

AUGUST

August 1
A fence stretching between states of mind,
rain worlds suspended from each barb.

A BRAND-NEW four-strand barbed-wire fence is being strung around sanctuary. These sixty acres run for several thousand feet along either side of the stream. The boundaries are rectangular, long and rather narrow for these enormous perspectives. Here where one can see for sixty or seventy miles this tiny plot of land consecrated as sanctuary serves as a state of mind for those who make contact with it. The fence rides the rolling hills and crosses the stream, angles down ravines, cuts across the far end of the cienega, then climbs again to hillcrest like a roller coaster. It creates the illusion of ownership, reflecting the ideation that creates nationality and war, a limitation of the psyche manifested in twirling strands of steel, wound every few inches with double metal prongs.

"Farmers were the original fence-builders of the world, and their fences were designed to keep animals and trespassers out. The very word 'fence' is taken from the word 'defense' which implies protection from an outside enemy. However, after it came into general use, barbed wire was used primarily to keep animals in! This controversial turnabout in the very concept of enclosure brought about some violent social and economic consequences in Arizona and other parts of the early West." (*Arizona Highways*, October 1969.)

For seven years this frontier homestead has been vacant of humans, reverting to the deer and the raccoon, the centipede and the snake. The rifle portholes cut in its thick walls, constructed to defend the original homesteaders from Indian attack, long since filled with fresh adobe to decrease the drafts. These walls, another form of fence, have kept man out while keeping him in, have protected man while excluding him, through his fears, from a more complete participation in his world. "Hope," someone said, "is a form of fear." And man's hope for survival is his fear of the present projected into the future. The wild imaginings of the mind gobble children like Moloch in a flaming pasture of scorpions, black widows and ten thousand asura-eyed rattlesnakes, when in reality we are beholding a thick green meadow lush as the palm of God.

> "As the main transcontinental railways cut through Arizona in the 1870s, they brought great benefits to this state's cattlemen in the form of increased market outlets . . . and availability of barbed wire. Glidden's wire, successfully marketed in 1874, was put to use locally the following year, after its merits had been demonstrated on the Great Plains.
>
> "Since that time barbed wire has remained firmly entwined with the development of the Arizona cattle industry. Despite the fact that it cut a bloody gash across the face of the land in the form of vicious range wars in the middle 1880s, it has played a vital part in the success of this important industry." (Ibid.)

Man fences the Unknown so that he may feel it subdued. So he uses language to define and therefore limit. He defines by stating limitations: we say something is five feet by five feet, or red, or deep, thereby saying what it isn't, a negativity; and this goes on into the endless spirals of thought-in-word that ends in an anthropomorphizing of God, limiting the unlimitable, slowly drawing closed all concepts like a bridge withdrawn from over a moat, sealing oneself off from ultimate reality. What man calls 'reason' may not be what 'brings him above the level of an animal', but indeed what separates him from rejoining the phyla of the world, able to crawl and fly with them, evolving in joy with them, with a recognition of what is occurring adding immensely to his growth and harmony. Instead we fence ourselves in with an arbitrary and subjective relativity we call 'logic', a place where reason is never allowed to lead us beyond itself.

"Prior to the introduction of the barb, smooth wire fencing was used for many years, but both its acceptance and success were limited. Barbed wire, too, surprisingly enough, was not readily accepted when it was first introduced. The chief reason, perhaps, was that livestock did not know to be wary of the barbs and were often injured by running into or through the wire. Injuries to livestock caused barbed wire to be classified as 'vicious', and led to the development of what was called the 'obvious' wire, a wide wire or strap that livestock could see more readily. In the years since, of course, livestock have learned to associate fence posts with barbed wire and thus protect their skins, and the once-vicious wire is now commonly used." (*Wildlife Views*, May-June 1969.)

On the second rise to the north of the house there are two deer trails that cross the fence, heading for the sweet waters of the stream. Until a month ago the old fence swayed and rusted in the wind. Crossing was a parlor trick, an easy crawl or jump, no obstacle. Now

58

that shining wire flies across the hills like a long thin swarm of metallic wasps. The deer stop at the wire, back up and prance toward it, then stop short. There is something not insurmountable but unnatural about this, a threat somewhere back in the hunter seasons of the memory. They cross elsewhere, still returning at dusk to the Rembrandt shadows bordering the soft green banks of the desert stream.

But if it is to be sanctuary, it cannot be 'ours': it must mean the land has been freed and returned to the planet.

The deer trails that once crossed the old fence fill slowly with grass and creeping mallow.

The fence that borders and defines the sanctuary, originally proposed as a defense against hunters and local cattle, becomes an offensive measure against that which it was meant to protect: the perfect circle once again, the equal and opposite forces of Newton's law of motion crystallized in human affairs. "That fence is meant to keep out man, the scourge," a sour-minded member of the Committee said. Cummings' 'manunkind' blisters in dark defense against the forces that each feels bubbling like magma just beneath the conscious surface of the mind. Jung with wirecutters defends the deer at sunset against the saber-toothed ancestors of our own Neolithic mud.

Each fence post is sunk two to three feet into the stony planet. Every fifteen feet the strands of wire are secured to the posts. Every five feet wire crosspieces keep the taut strands parallel, nearly immovable, seemingly permanent. Along slight depressions beneath the wire the trails of javelina, fox, coyote, rabbit, skunk and raccoon pass freely.

August 4   *Deer trail, matted grass, a birth bed.*

White-tailed deer thread their way through the oak forest and along the stream silently as mice in a dark kitchen. Does deliver fawns in cattailed refuge near willow thicket sunshade haven. Bucks 'in the velvet', white tails wagging. Last November's rutting battles come to fruition, we watch pregnant doe test each step through tall grass to disappear delicately into lattice-work of coyote willow toward the most natural of childbirths, alone and slightly changing. Each being sniffs the air and mates in holy gusto. The perfect circle completed perfectly to the tune hummed by the invisible host beaming in our chromosomes.

August 7

These first six weeks of sanctuary have been ironic reflections of the Aquarian Age. The Water Bearer has been the center of our life mandala. Though lightning owns the sky of the first great summer downpours, water has been the focus of our existence. The well possessed for the past seven years by the birds and animals of the area is now unusable by our human species. Drinking water carried in gallon containers from a gracious neighbor.

The sixty acres that comprise the sanctuary form a long rectangle running north and south like a migra-

60

tory corridor. O'Donnell Creek, the year-round stream that creates this unique oasis, its roots underground in the Canelo Hills, surfaces two miles to the south in the rusting savannah, flowing through sanctuary to feed and sustain this wilderness paradise. This stream is one of the unique aspects of the sanctuary; to maintain it and the cienega we are building the dam. It will protect groundwaters from dropping, halting any further siphoning of the precious waters from the streamside marsh. By building this soil-retention dam the cienega, perhaps the best living example of this ecological form in southern Arizona, will be allowed to survive. Without the dam the stream would cut a trench down to bedrock and drain the cienega completely, as evidenced by drying streambeds throughout Arizona. Once flanked by miles of lush cienegas now extinct, the streams cut their banks ten, fifteen, twenty feet down to bedrock, their pebbly courses exposed to the white sun except in the rainy season when torrents careen through deep-cut channels and chase life to the rim.

Early in the week an extraordinarily heavy rain fell, three inches in less than an hour. The rain had just abated when we went from the house down the path skirting the marsh to the stream to see how the cutback was faring under this increased water flow. At the waterfall, where the ten foot drop to the pool had changed the level of the streambed, a slightly heavier flow expanded the grandeur, continuing downstream between steep banks. In the past as the waters tore over the waterfall's soft edge the ledge was cut back, receding upstream to continue the deep cutting of the banks, further endangering the cienega. But now even with the increased pressure from the rain there seemed no imminent danger and we suspected that the cutback would be able to withstand the monsoon.

The rain had begun and ceased in less than an hour; everything seemed fine. We turned to walk back to the house but just as we approached the porch we heard behind us the crest of a tremendous overflow crashing down the streambed, a wave perhaps two feet high, powerful enough to carry tree trunks fifty feet out into the cienega, cracking willows, tearing out walnut trees, dismembering exposed roots of cottonwoods. In minutes the whole area was inundated in one overwhelming rush of water. It was what local inhabitants call a fifty year flood, which we were later told struck at fifty-two hundred cubic feet per second. A cubic foot of water weighs in excess of sixty-two pounds, the pressure on the waterfall rim many tons per square inch. Under more natural circumstances where the runoff would have been a slow accumulation, feeding stream and tree and allowing life to pass along the artery downhill to pool and cienega, the stream might have accommodated this amount of rain. But these natural conditions had long since been altered by years of grazing and tree cutting. The water ripped through the stream bottom tearing away the soil, and within the next two hours the cutback receded one hundred and fifty feet upstream, leaving below it a tangle of walnut, ash, and cottonwood limbs like a sunken galleon lying on its side. The early workings on the dam dispossessed, like the tiny native fish thrown downstream by the first torrential wave.

And yet through the Southwest there is a drying trend; a growth of man-made desert marching slowly and steadily uphill, ocatillo, mesquite, prickly pear and cacti invading higher altitudes as the climate becomes hotter and drier. This is a result of many factors, perhaps beginning with the overgrazing of the 1870s and 1880s resulting in the great arroyo-cutting that culminated in the three year drought of the 1890s which left half a million cattle dead on the range. Climatic changes occur as open stretches of ground, overgrazed and exposed to the sun, absorb more heat drying the springs rising there. The tree cover removed by the clear cutting of forests or the removal of plant life in a watershed; the ground heated and yet less water available; the streams diverted for irrigation above the marshes which baked dry as cow skull in the white Southwestern sun; the great marsh grasses and tules replaced by desert shrubbery. Where once tall grasses and deep-rooted trees drank in the rains raising the water table and slowing the runoff, tremendous flash floods have ruined the fragile stream networks. The rains become a catastrophe rather than a boon, washing away topsoil with cresting tumults that shatter the streambeds and cut to bedrock. The juniper descends from higher altitudes to take its place as one more milestone of imbalance, crowding the native grasses and shrubs. The destruction has been led by man, consumer of the irreplaceable water and wildlife of the Southwest; the shallow lakes and beaver dams, the once luxuriant marshes, cienegas and ponds, now dry desert progressing higher and higher against the retreating oaks. This trend could eventually turn the whole

Southwest to desert. In Tucson the water level steadily declines and it is quite common to drill wells deeper every few years.

Perhaps the waters were once kept above ground by the net of biological activity that existed before the intervention of man: the microorganisms acting as a kind of sealer of organic debris, a constantly renewed life system cementing the streambed and soil allowing the water to flow from the surface of the land. Now the water disappears and streambeds remain dry as shed snakeskin. The intricate net of life disturbed: water in the Southwest becoming more precious and less obtainable each year.

Anyone who has walked an arroyo during the beginnings of a rainstorm knows well enough what a flash flood means. I have more than once scrambled out of an arroyo accompanied by a rat or javelina or fox seeking higher ground, only to observe the water come crashing down as though released from an uphill sluice just minutes after the rain has begun. I have seen cars overturned and heard of people drowned, not quick enough to elude this modern catastrophe of soil, air and water unbalanced by greed. Flash floods are the result of flash thinking, of not seeing deeply enough. The arroyos cut into the flesh of the planet seem directly related to the flesh of the cattle drawn out of the native grasses until both reach the point of extinction: the cattle find it less habitable, the grasses disappear. And Arizona is running out of water. There is talk of piping water down from the Northwest, but it is doubtful that the water control agencies in Washington and Oregon, courted with equal ardor by the yellow industrial smogslick that is Los Angeles, will be receptive. If it were not for the dam the stream would soon be a dry seasonal trickle—a trench, another arroyo, through whose soft walls would have drained the waters of this rich cienega, its mud cracking and baking like the surrounding bone-dry hillsides: the sedge and tule gone, the migratory birds seeking green haven further south. Without the dam, no stream; without the stream, no cienega. Without the cienega, no oasis: no unique breeding ground; no special place to expand the concepts which 'civilization' leaves unfulfilled, that aspect of man which is drained away in the mechanization of the city. And so this relic geological formation of wet meadow, the marshy cienega, continues to enhance our lives; and though we may never see it, we would yet sense its extinction as one might feel the loss of a distant relative.

August 10   *Dam called on account of rain.*

The sun descends behind wolfbacked hills, settling into its nest in the Santa Rita Mountains, paralleling Mexico in the firesweep sky.

The dam back to the drawing board. Ten days of cutback in the stream tearing out larger portions of the streamside woodland have caused us to reorganize our efforts on the dam. Riprap to be used to reinforce the downstream walls of the creek. The wingwalls poured remain, tied solidly into the outcropping of rock on either side of the intended dam. The rains have abated; water flows thinly where a few days ago a river torrential beyond recollection of all local residents carved its fifty year discontent in the ancient memory of mineral and microbe. So far our efforts at planet plumbing unsuccessful in halting change, out of which all evolution is born. Newly exposed ridges of clay and rock curl and twist, presenting new waterfall dimensions grander than expected: Nature creating great beauty in change, though threatening in its magnificence another manifestation of her grace, the cienega.

August 12   *A unicorn's green eyes in a gentle summer rain; griffins in the cottonwoods.*

The waters have retreated from the cienega, leaving a silence in the wake of this great natural force which reminds one of the calm following an intense physical experience. Tara naked on a rope swing, humming to the greater mind.

August 13   *Planet plumbing resumed; huge trucks each morning with breakfast.*

In the increased activity of work on the dam the sounds of the great machines send us visiting neighbors. A few miles down the dusty road toward Mexico live our neighbors and patriarchal friends the Mellors, whose Canelo Hills Ranch provided us with our horses and many extraordinary introductions to the social life of the Southwest. Having left a Philadelphia bookstore business ten years before to come to Arizona to raise horses and their eight children, the Mellors became our guides to the ecology of cacti, cowboy, horse, and Chicano in the warm roundtable ranch house suppers which we were occasionally to attend. They took us under their wing as an addition to their already large family, becoming our very close friends. Cassie smiling in her fifties, hair short to the sun, robust, and everactive—though there were those elbows-on-the-table, third-cup-of-coffee, fifth-cigarette mornings when she just couldn't seem to get going . . . and why should she, after all, having done so much already? And Clint, fifty years old, silver hair cut close to his sun-browned scalp, a javelin of stone, thin and sinuous as an Indian, welcoming us and offering us lunch as though we had been expected. Sitting at the ranch house table speaking of the concepts of sanctuary, all creatures gaining new light within the minds of neighboring cowboys and cattlemen. Cowbird, primrose, porcupine, and human acquire new meaning during a pleasant day with new friends. The society of the Southwest somewhat different than our city experience, a hospitality of freshly baked bread and open-armed communication. For us another form of sanctuary—close friendship with newly met people who open their house to us and sincerely wish us to feel at home. Offering an alternative social relationship where friendships develop quickly, like a flower opening from a ready bud, we enter into their family as one of the tribe, no less cared for or with any less concern than for their own. A remarkable experience of humans in contact, trusting as deer.

August 14   *Jaguar on the pampas of Patagonia.*

Every few years an old male cat comes over the mountains out of Mexico like Hemingway's panther on Kilimanjaro, coming to the fatted flanks of America. Each time one appears he is hunted and taken as trophy to man's imagined possession of the land. Today another was shot a few miles west, hunted like the 'wetback' immigrants (locally termed the 'cousins') who use this basin as pathway to the north.

At one time the course of this stream was part of a hundred mile wolf run coming out of Mexico heading west to the Patagonia Mountains, turning south to the San Rafael Valley and into the foothills of the Mexican mountains to complete the circle. Now the wolves are gone, except for a few eluding the sharpshooters in dens in the Huachuca and Catalina Mountains, and only an occasional jaguar comes to be killed. A menace, they say, like the 'cousins' who come through sanctuary looking for hard work, declining unearned sandwiches until sparse communication is made through the slow-tongued efforts of my pidgin Spanish. They smile and join our family on the porch, eluding midday sun for a moment before passing on toward Tucson. Bare brown feet on bare brown earth.

August 15   *A brown thrasher whistles at my
               'uniform' as I saddle Duster.*

The ranger badge I have been asked by the Committee to wear during the upcoming deer season is a bit of absurd theater, since I would never arrest anyone or have them arrested. Instead I will attempt to instill some sense of the interlocking nature of all beings. And here I am, Officer Antares, saying put down your gun and come in for a beer. This is sanctuary; we do not kill here, we watch.

Now I am Yogi-Cowboy-Guide-and-Planet Ranger, feeling something like Father Earth with wife, daughter, mother and pup, mare and filly, mockingbird fledgling and all the free-flung creatures of the universe under my psychic protection. The Committee has suggested I carry a firearm during hunting season, for 'protection' from the likes of rabid animals and drunken hunters. I have told them that a gun is a second spine which generates a false self-esteem and acts as an antenna for negative actions, precipitating rather than deterring violence. They agree, with some hesitation. I suggest a stun gun for rabid animals or those which need to be relocated to the safer back country; for alcohol-warmed hunters, kindness may suffice. They agree once again with a bit more light in their eyes, having been offered a more positive alternative in keeping with the concept of sanctuary. They seem to love this place though they are yet quite possessive about 'their' sanctuary, which is not theirs or ours but is instead the planet's.

August 17   *A cienegafire of wildflowers.*

New blossoms appear daily in the cienega. The summer rains germinate a history of seeds. Yellow composites everywhere. Some species flower for just a day or two then disappear again for another year. There are flowers here that only someone present daily on the land might see. Constant rebirth stamined and pistilled with the wands and rafts that carry one to the hidden shore; the greenness becoming almost blue near the cattailed springs that shelter deer and mulberry, fawn and seedling. The walnuts begin their descent from a hundred trees beside the stream. Grapes drape and curl about fallen trees whose taking from the soil is now reversed in the constant replenishment of the cycle undisturbed. Beans yellow in their sheaths, dangling from the fossil leafwings of the deep-rooted mesquite. Once-cultivated asparagus gone free, a volunteer like us all, picks its living place, delicately extending lacy branches reminiscent of the dill and anise that abound in the foggy California hills from which we have come.

A great blue heron with a wingspan greater than mine lifts himself from the marsh over cottonwoods into greenness beyond.

August 18

Time for me to go back and read/experience the writings and human magics of St. Francis of Assisi. Talk with animals once again returned to the dream-realities of child-clear thought. It is out of such thinking, I suspect, that Lao Tzu came upon the Tao of his teachings.

From among the primroses, buttercups, and blue-eyed grass rises the rare delicate white orchid known as lady's tresses (*Spiranthes graminia*) along the western periphery of the cienega. Tiny white baroque trumpet flowers spiral up the dark green stem making their debut today, coincident with the profuse blue sorrel on the outcropping by the quince. Not seen since 1938, thought extinct in this country, this rare orchid was rediscovered after the Nature Conservancy secured this land to preserve its delicate ecosystem: another creature protected at sanctuary, rather than added as a delicacy to the appetites of the neighboring cows grazing on the less verdant hillsides where yesterday the white star lily appeared as dessert instead.

August 20   *"We walk on the roof of Hell*
                               gazing at the flowers"
                               wishing we had a camera.

The camera was one of the first time-machines. It locks in space happenstances of another moment. It is capable of recreating the past, bringing forward a vibratory frequency of light and form, spirit and emotion, long since arisen and passed away.

Matthew Brady, like Dante, was capable of descending through time to the personifications of the darkest forces of the mind crystallized in his chosen emulsion . . . Dante chose language as his image-sensitive medium; the difference is nearly one of metaphor. War, like love, draws on the most base and divine resources; to show this is to uncover the molten center to the creature.

The rains have raised the water table; water stands in the cienega. The hard dry hills gone moist with fresh grasses and new flowers everywhere. My camera and I going out for walks daily to witness the upsurge of dormant life, recording the moisture and clocking the sun. Each day something new to photograph. Each day fresh blossoms on the hillsides or beside the stream. The reds, yellows, blues, whites, pinks, purples and oranges of new flowers attracting a closeup view of the fecund planet. Like film, the mind imprints this rapid ongoing explosion of life everywhere about us.

August 21   *The Kingbird Burial.*

In green meadow Bob and I
picking apples pears quince
offered by frontiersman
buried 80 years
beneath the porch.

The barking of one of the dogs
attracting us through shoulderhigh
Johnson grass, bordering walnut trees
and across the stream, up the side
of an outcropping of lichened rock
into the miniature forest of
twisted live oak
where we see dog

        sitting barking tailwagging
having treed a coatimundi
whose two foot tail swishing
at first makes me think
he has cornered a puma
but long snout swings our way,
the chattering of denial and warning
shaking the limb
his catround eyes staring into mine
in plea and survival threat
though he can easily destroy this dog
so gleefully awaiting my praise—
instead the harsh edge of my voice
lowers dog's ears against furry head
crouching confused
scolded in the warm green shade of victory
in which he stands conqueror
            pulled away
allowing coatimundi, large tropical relative
of raccoon, to
bound to higher ground
in safety of grandfather oak
chattering in the midst of sanctuary.

We return to the house
to discover in a dictionary
the beautiful derivation
of this golden creature,
the first one we have met.
And I go into the Bird Room
to feed the second bird
we have taken in—

The first a mockingbird
found beneath thunder apple tree
in the midst of first summerrains
long since freed
          though still about
flying from treetop
to our shoulders for a shirtpocket raisin
fed a dozen times a day
another member of the Planet Family.
The latest charge a wounded Cassin's kingbird
brought by a neighbor
nearly two days before,
shot by his 11 year old brother
          with a BB gun
the wing bones broken
          the flesh torn beneath left wing
just this morning beginning to gentle a bit
nearly taking a piece of hamburger
and raisin offered.
Now dead—
still warm
passed from his body
less than an hour before
found stilled on his side
as I stand there   speechless
picking him up, taking him outside
into flightless space
to bury him.
Walking toward the stream,
tears absorbed in high mountain desert,
his back nestled against my palm
his yellow breast turned upward

74

to the empty sky.
Reminding me of the yellow flesh
of ten thousand children burning
in the jungles of Viet Nam.
Reminding me that what killed this bird
    kills man
that the trigger finger mind
seeking to prove itself
in the death of another
is the suicide of consciousness,
the dissociation
    of man from nature, removed
from his lifestuff percolating through.
That what killed this slowly stiffening bird
    kills the planet
    kills itself
as guileful as Pavlov
in the fascism of its loves,
    conquers man
locking him in the least realms of mind,
anchored to the bleeding foetus of his fears:
blocked from the light of the living continuum
in which he might find his joy . . .
The bird laid to rest
in the limbcrotch of old cottonwood
beside the stream, covered with dead bark
of ancient willow
       (all white buffalos absent)
left to return
to that from which he sprang.

August 22   *Tara stands alone, her voyage*
                               well underway.

A crippled white-winged dove brought home with
me from an expedition downstream, found on the open
range. The wing bone broken—cardboard splint taped
over the injury, the wing supported to an anchor tape
around the body, he is fed and watered, then put into
the Bird Room for rest and recuperation. Charlie One
Wing, plump relative of the European rock dove commonly known as a pigeon, exterior decorator of city
ledges and statues, emits a frightened coo of thanks
as the door quietly closes leaving him to heal.

August 23   *Horsing around with Duster.*

The day began with oats and grain, raking the corral,
changing water, combing, applying mineral oil and
kerosene to huge mosquito welts on Duster's flank
then saddling her for a long ride atop the mesa. Duster's speed increasing in direct proportion to the care
and concern she is receiving. Her seven week old filly
keeps a good pace alongside us, kicking her heels and
calling back and forth to her mother of the freedom of
seventy mile visibility and the majesty of the purple
planet rim.

August 24   *Clouds totalize the sky.*

Lightning through the morning, rain through the

afternoon. The birds are quiet, resting beneath the widespread leaves of new summer foliage. A very quiet day indoors.

August 25   *A flash of indigo in the apple trees.*

Fumbling through my Peterson's guide to identify the deep blues and orange of this tenor lovesong, a blue grosbeak and mate flirting through branches hung heavy with ripening apples. Adam and Eve in another incarnation?
Mexican jays gathering noisily by the stream.

August 26   *Jays congregating for the second day; migration?*

This morning there are silver furrows in the sky stretching twenty miles above the Huachuca Mountains dissolving into the Southwestern blue ether. Birds chutting heeking swutting jigjigjigjigging. Songs from the cottonwoods near the house. Apples, pears and quince picked from unsprayed windpruned Godwatered trees. Outlaw Fyodor munching green apples stolen from the kitchen last night, a tummyache today for sure. Wild asparagus, grapes, watercress, mulberry, mesquite bean, cattail, various edible cacti, manzanita berries, yellow currant, black walnuts, gourd squash, and sweet acorns are on the menu of the continuum.

August 27   *A week of orchids ended.*

The last orchid pressed and put in the refrigerator, cold as a fossil, to be picked up by one of the Committee for post mortem at the University of Arizona.

August 28

Rain, then berry-sized hail, all arroyos running, javelina seeking higher ground: the human family high and dry by the fireplace.

August 29   *Great blue heron at dawn while saddling.*

Whitewing dove, bird of peace, fledged back to the wild on the day before dove season. Wing mended a bit low, a lopsided sideswing to the south; then circling back again for a day or two of handouts, not strong enough to migrate, allowed to mend at sanctuary in the grasslands of the hill rising behind the house. The whole sanctuary a healing nest protected from the shotguns oiled on Tucson's kitchen tables.

SEPTEMBER

September 1
The kingbird dead, Charlie One Wing free,
the mockingbird nowhere to be seen.

WALKING ACROSS the thick greenness of the cienega, the soles of my boots sunk into the black richness of the life-supporting mud, I am Man, the leading edge of consciousness in the tune-scale of evolution—the first Song Master of the Phyla, custodian-guide to this recent state of mind designated as Sanctuary.

The rains were just beginning to fall in mid-July when we heard the frightened squawk of a fallen nestling. Beneath thunder apple tree in the increasing downpour a wet scraggly week-old mockingbird chick was hopping about while mother swooped above, unable to return her lost babe to the bulky nest of twigs and weed stems so well hidden we could not find it.

First we took the bird inside. Then, thinking mother mockingbird might find a way, we waited until the intense rains had abated and returned the chick to its finding place. On the porch a few hundred feet away we watched through binoculars while the mother attempted to feed and shelter her offspring from the inevitable darkness and the prowling of countless 'natural enemies', those who naturally sought this bird for their sustenance—the skunk, the snake, the hawk, the badger, the coyote, the ringtail, the bobcat; and all the unknowns waiting in some drying niche or nest, with stomachs growling in wind- and rain-drenched hunger. Mother could only attempt to bluff away these fellow wildlings in hopes of her chick's survival. She might stay through the night swooping and pecking as she did at our dogs when they sniffed out the babe nearly an hour later, when we returned to see if the protection of our house and our care might not be of greater aid.

We put the frightened nestling in our daughter's unused playpen to spend the night in a room of its own.

The first afternoon, nothing—sitting in a corner, milk-soaked kibbled dog food and seeds refused.

The next day we spent much time together, sitting in that bare room squinting and cocking our heads at each other. Then the irrepressible desire for food broke through and the bird was sitting in my palm, beak cranked wide open, a funnel cheeping and tchacking at me to supply the necessary sustenance.

The mockingbird is a plagiarist, one of the 'mimic thrushes'. An extraordinary linguist, he often orchestrates the songs of other species into an original creation of the first magnitude. *Mimus polyglottos*: strong-legged, long-tailed, yellow-eyed, with a black, slightly recurved bill. Food: beetles, grasshoppers and other insects, fruit, grape and holly preferred. Protein, water, calcium, vitamins.

That second day, perched on my finger, he accepted very lean hamburger and whole wheat bread with up-tilted wide-open beak. Then bananas and more water-soaked bread; more hamburger. Hotdogs wisely refused. Plums, peaches, a commercial fledgling food of seeds, eggs and grains accepted heartily. A preference for chicken and bananas, water from his own cup, a piece of moist red-purple plum, an ironic bit of turkey stuffing, breads made with stone-ground flour.

By the end of the week we were waking with the sun to the insistent tchacking of our newest tribal member, requesting breakfast and fresh water. Eleven month old wide-eyed Tara reaching up shyly to say good morning to this grey-white fluffy brother. Each day a growing communication, 'the Mocker' flying to the door to greet me as I entered the Bird Room with fresh food—no longer staying in the playpen, now able to fly to his favorite roost atop a wide-mouth stained-glass apothecary jar on the window sill. Sitting alone with this growing seven inch long fellow being, talking quietly to him as he flew from his roost to the top of my head, jumping down onto my shoulder to peck playfully at my long hair, making a new, very low chuck-chucking sound near my ear. Taking me for a mate. "He probably thinks he's a human being. Or that you're a mockingbird," a visiting ecologist from the Nature Conservancy says one day. There is a real communication coming about between birdsoul and humansoul, addressing one another directly, finding no real difference.

Because our three month old dinosaur-footed shepherd pup is named Li Po after the drunken God-visioned sixth century Chinese poet, we thought that 'the Mocker' might be named Tu Fu, Li Po's sober-minded court-poet contemporary—for no particular reason of characteristics. A week later Patricia, writing a letter to a friend, called the bird 'tofu', which is Japanese beancake—a more apt name which stuck. 'Beancake' and I immediately accepted its ironic reasonableness.

By mid-August Beancake was fat and flying well: time for him to go out and follow his genetic directive. One Saturday morning when we awoke with the arrival of our first visitors from the greater family of San Francisco, having intended to let him back into the sky this day, Beancake was already gone: 'escaped' through a space at the bottom of a weather-beaten door which the puppy Li Po had broken through in his drunken play, attempting to meet this distant birdfellow. Outside, the dogs sat like spectators at a tennis match, watching the bird fly between the roofs of the two adobe buildings: pushing against the greatest expanse of air he had yet known, his wingbeats perhaps a bit more rapid than need be, more like a dove than a gliding night songster, tchack-tchacking to us of his liberation. Free, at play, though still in communication; flying down to the ground to hop about us chuckling, then up onto the roof, back to the ground near us, back to the roof, then onto my head; balancing, stretching his wings, flicking his rudder-tail.

He came into the kitchen with us for breakfast, then went back out into the oak beside the house. When we came out onto the porch he was sitting on the porch roof peering down over the edge at us, fluttering down for food and recreation several times during the day. Within a few days he was following our hikes down to the stream or out on a photographic expedition, flying from tree to tree above us, coming down to sit in the open-topped viewer of my double reflex camera, chuckling and obstructing my view. Then riding home with me down the hill, a great lazy bird in a conquered camera nest; waiting for a raisin or two from my shirt pocket, then up into a tree to do a tail-balancing act like an oriental fan dancer and warm himself in the yellow summer sun.

By the end of the week he was knocking on the window for food and lodging, dropping out of a tree onto the heads of astonished visitors to chirp for food and have his picture taken, or to sit quietly for a moment should that head belong to some unnamed good vibration who might tchack back at him—landing sometimes near the dogs, but keeping one hop ahead of them; quicker than they, but with many solo hours still to be logged before complete survival maneuverability would be attained.

Soon there were times when the Mocker flew off by himself to chase his instincts through the trees. Occasionally, while sitting in a tree, he would cock his head to eye a genetically reminiscent insect, pecking at it and trying to swallow this 'uncivilized' food. Growing in his natural aptitudes, though filled with the thought of man as his benefactor, vociferous and open in his trust. While Beancake learned and remembered, the Bird Room was reoccupied by the wounded Cassin's kingbird: an individualistic bird often seen harassing hawks and ravens above the stream, family named Tyrannus for its fierce personality. His polished ebony eye glistening with fear and defense. His shiny black bill biting me hello as I placed him in the protective playpen, unwilling to take food until just before his final dull-eyed death.

The Kingbird laid to rest, the passing of some part of us. The Mocker did not follow this cortege but stayed on the porch, flying over to the apple tree from which he had fallen five weeks before.

Wednesday night the Mocker asked to be let in the house. He stayed in the again vacant Bird Room for the first time in five days.

Thursday morning Beancake ate and left for a while, returning in an hour or so for food and the continuance of the ongoing family scene. That night, because we were bidding our visiting friends goodbye the next morning, we decided to drive to Tucson for a farewell supper at a favorite restaurant. Friday morning when we arose, the Mocker was nowhere about. We have not seen him since.

Our minds have never been so absorbed in any single recollection. Each bird is observed more closely than ever before; each twert and whistle computed against the steady possibility of recognition, like a parent listening for a child's voice in a crowded room.

Then just before sunset, a Cooper's hawk swoops low above the house and the fear explodes that the hawk may have carried off our friend the evening before. The experience of talons ripping my flesh recurs before and during sleep; the talons wrap about me, burning into my chest as they lift me screaming from the ground, the great predator's head turning toward me like an Aztec priest to tear my heart from my body.

The first experience upon rising is the keen listening for the Mocker's tchack. Orioles, cardinals, flycatchers, the acorn woodpecker . . . no mockingbirds. All day I listen, reflecting, while pulling juniper fence posts from the body of the cienega, freeing her to return to her more natural course. I am utterly absorbed in this absent member of the family, our link with every other sentient creature included in this miraculous union which occurred and passed away so quickly. Transience. Attachment. The impermanence out of which all sorrow is born; the very real suffering that the mind brings forth in response to unfulfilled desire.

The next day, too, no Mocker. My mind finding the most steady concentration it had ever experienced on the thought of this bird. A total absorption, a one-pointedness never quite achieved in my meditations. The thought-form of this bird is as clear as an apparition. There is an astonishing ability to associate the missing bird with every object or flash of movement, reminding me of God-graced Ramakrishna's comment that if one thought steadily of Christ or Krishna for three days he would find Him. But what of the constant thought-recollection-desire for this slight bird? Would not the meditation on Christ or Krishna be a better use of this mental activity? But the magnetism of this bird continues, like the planet's effect on a compass or a holy mountain's effect on a pilgrim, an awkward, often painful steadiness of the mind that will not be shaken, much like that of Tibetan tanka scroll painters who will not look at any other images but those which it is their life's work to reproduce over and over, dakinis and demons, bodhisattvas and buddhas, heaven and hell.

There is, I think to myself, the possibility that the bird may have flown off to find its life in the world of birds—a comforting alternative to the intermittent talons of fear. Or he may be molting silently nearby. Or he may have been chased off by his parents when they saw he was able to get about, an instinctive territorial defense. There is a great irony in the fact that this bird's instinctual reactions were considerably distorted by his having taken humans for parents: his song, usually reserved for territorial threat-chant or mating call, become for him a love- and chow-call to his strange biped companions. He may well have been simply 'misunderstood' by his species, an outsider in the bird world.

On the fourth day the ear and eye find a new modulation, a new awareness born of a new experience of all that soars and flutters, chirps and calls. There comes an insight into the passing nature of the lifestuff, into the ten thousand forms of the One, divided, decorated and painted, gilled and feathered, furred and clawed, the Planet Family of which we are all members. And I recall a story about a great sage who upon death was passing from his body through the realms and bardos of the Other Side; and just upon reaching the top of this final journey, just as he was about to get off the karmic wheel, he thought of a forest doe he had been tending and wondered of its welfare, and was immediately reborn as a deer.

For the past two days Tara has been looking up in the air, following an unseen flight from sill to table to rafter above my head. It is all too easy to believe she sees that bird's spirit. She has not done this before and she dearly loved that bird, sat entranced for long intervals watching him eat or fly or roost, holding out a flat self-conscious palm for him to land upon, letting him rest on her bald head the day before he disappeared. She smiles sometimes at the ghost above us. Perhaps she sees our intense thought-forms, our desire for Beancake's safety. Perhaps she sees that fellow above us, no longer hungry though still around in mutual attachment, yet to pass on to some untouchable world.

Today there is a great gathering of birds about the house: woodpeckers, sparrows, finches, warblers and flycatchers. It is an extraordinary day, life-consciousness like a dome over the sanctuary. The initiation completed; undertaking our responsibilities as planet stewards.

September 2   *Watching man rope himself from saddleback.*

Sixteen miles northeast of sanctuary on the way to Tucson is the Sonoita crossroads. Although the county of Santa Cruz in which we live is the smallest county in Arizona, it has a typically large county fairground, used for everything from local beauty pageants to rodeos and stock shows.

Today is the day of the Santa Cruz County Rodeo and we go reluctantly to see our past hog-tied in the hot Southwestern dust. Yip, holler, and hooray, our cloven selves bellowing for respite. The earth baked hard as terracotta where in the 1850s the well-known border surveyor Bartlet recorded his wagons bogged down in the muds of an immense cienega, already parched dry by 1888, the time of the first grandstand rodeo competition in Prescott.

Driving home at dusk a local cowboy tells us that for all the dust and fury rodeo riders almost never get killed in rodeos; they die instead on the road, in station wagons, driving all night to get to the next event.

September 3   *A poet, like a policeman,*
                            is always on duty.

A car passes the house without stopping, heading toward the stream. We walk down the path and approach their picnic blanket, asking their purpose. "We are friends of the Committee," they reply; "we were told we could picnic here." We remind them that the Committee does not own this land but has only been selected to supervise its protection, and that sanctuary is not anyone's personal playground. No collecting; put that butterfly net back in its holster. Enjoy the wildlings alive—take your killjars with you, they're bad for business!

September 4

Letter today from the gentle city-sanga of the Tibetan Lama who, through a long chain of spiritual coincidences had named our daughter, Tara, from halfway around the earth a year before we met him when he arrived in the United States. Now mutual friends are sitting as his students in Berkeley, writing us of the good things coming forth from Rimpoche's energies. To sit and be someone's disciple again . . . but the planet keeps reminding me just to be silent here, beside a stream, in the early morning gayatri-sun, in the midst of the marsh during summer rain, surrounded by short-lived wildflowers or beneath an ancient cottonwood.

The Earth, Mother Durga, is ticklish and another hunting season has just begun. Fluttering doves are plucked from the sky by Remington shotguns and stuffed into automobiles fed on the fossil blood of Mother Planet, hung like sagging testicles upon the prideblind shoulder. Wife and kids wag their tails at daddy's killer residue, applauding ancient genetic hangovers to the whistling steam of the pressure cooker while feathers mold in a city dump. But all this is passing. One way or another man will see his spirit reflected in the eyes of his brothers—and in each blade of grass, as the bodhisattva's vow goes. It is up to us whether this will occur, whether we can transcend the clumsy human game of master and slave, protection and murder.

September 5   *Planet as tutelary deity, our*
                      teacher, brings us back to
                      our senses.

Our spiritual discipline has become simply a will to be still and centered, to be able to experience freshly, beyond conditioning, to see each moment as it arises. I am beginning to find that all I really want to do is talk-respond-interact with the wilderness of the mind manifest in coatimundi, eagle, porcupine, mockingbird, dove, kingbird, horse, dog, wife and child. It is like Krishna saying to Arjuna, "I have had ten thousand lives; so have you. The difference between us is that I know mine and you do not know yours." Perhaps these ten thousand rebirths are simultaneous—perhaps they exist at once (and yet forever) and are capable of being contacted now, everywhere. To seek communication with animals is to make contact with our genes, one of our forms, another aspect of ourselves, of our rebirths. I see a commune of animal speakers, of vegetarian brothers; a commune of planet consciousness, in the rule of Tao. Not a dream but something to be worked toward: dreamt into action, made to become real.

I think when we have been here awhile I will be able to talk with the animals, to understand the mockingbirds and cicadas. This is not what is described as 'enlightenment', but it attracts those same tendencies.

September 9   *A flower's flickering greeting.*

From the green mossy banks of the stream rises the incredibly red cardinal flower, lobelia, cousin of Indian tobacco, the sacrament of greeting and contemplation undulating in the breeze of the Apache Southwest. The scarlet blossom appearing, like the single candle on Tara's cake, to celebrate her first birthday.

September 10   *A meeting with remarkable men.*

To Tucson to meet with ecologists from the University of Arizona at the home of Bill Woodin, director of the Arizona-Sonora Desert Museum. Joseph Wood Krutch and a few of the more concerned professionals

93

from the Committee address my questions about what might be learned of talking with animals. We discuss at length the native American shamans and wilderness seekers, the animal speakers. They are silent at first, coming only slowly to the surface, conditioned by learning in a certain way. We speak of the work of Konrad Lorenz on the language of animals, having noted the different interpretations birds give songs and gestures. Lorenz has observed subtle differences between the call for long-distance flight and that for a shorter flight; jackdaws, a European relative of the crow, are capable by the slightest intonation to communicate to the other birds in the flock the distance they are considering traveling. Certainly this is the language of animals, something to be learned by close association and respect, by watching and listening.

Later we trade organic, unpoisoned, windpruned, earthfed pears, apples and quince for raw sugar, peppermint tea, brown rice, whole wheat flour and sunflowerseed oil at a natural food store called Aquarian Farmery; a few books of my poetry at the adjoining Gayatri bookshop for a Tao Te Ching, Conze translations of Buddhist scriptures, and Eisley's *Immense Journey.*

September 11   *Fyodor strikes again.*

   Typewriter malfunction—erratic spacing, keys sticking, the action jammed with a few ounces of bird seed smuggled from the next door Bird Room and sequestered in the typewriter by our nefarious yellow-eyed friend.

94

September 12

The dogs' noses and tongues bristle with porcupine quills. I sit down quietly with each dog in the end room, clipping the tip of each quill to break its suction before pulling the shafts out with a pair of pliers. A long morning, then to the vet for antibiotics, returning to a solar eclipse as the pile driver begins slamming the new well into the hard earth. Well driller Comanche Bill, honcho of his own rig, a wildcatter migrated from the oil fields of Oklahoma, tells us of fossil waters "trapped there since it all solidified," which he wishes not to tap as so many do in the drying Southwest, continuing on his way through strata of earth's history toward an ample supply of water for use in the house. He shows us clippings from *Life* magazine, pictures of him riding his zebra ten years ago in the rodeo. A rodeo man for twenty years, with a sore back and hard hands, tapping the capillaries of the mother planet in bib overalls and embroidered French cuffs.

September 14   *Comanche Bill caps at one hundred and forty feet.*

Displacing the silence of the work finished on the well, gunfire near the northern fence. I go to investigate but find only three spent cartridges, a cigarette butt and some broken feathers. Tire tracks disappear onto the open range seeking other poaching.

September 16

This afternoon I rode Duster to hang the first No Hunting signs on the new fence, saddlebags slung over her fine humpend holding signs, wire for hanging, and pliers for twisting signs tight to the shiny ominous barbed wire. Completed southern and eastern fences and part of western rolling fence, crossing the stream on Duster after many reluctant turnings, then jumping the shallow waters a few hundred feet downstream from the cutback and on up the hill where we saw the coatimundi flipping stones in search of tasty morsels. Near the clusters of blue oaks, at the edge of the thickly flowered field northeast of the house, band-tailed pigeons flutter out of a streamside walnut; Duster only mildly interested in their flight pattern. Her filly, Cienega, dances in the tall sedge. Li Po recites some forgotten limerick to himself, nose in the high grass, tail thrashing like a dull scythe, snuffling in the rich earth. Back to the house by sunset, horses grained and returned to the field with tails swishing. And I sit down to write old friends of how it is here in paradise.

September 18   *Liberating the cienega.*

Removing more of the old juniper fence posts and last century's 'copper plate' barbed wire, one of the first types patented, allowing the 'expansion of the West'. A battered Sharps buffalo rifle barrel used as a fence support near the spring rusts in the intricate shadow of the willow-thickets' gracious shade.

September 21   *Autumnal equinox. Water*
                             consciousness in the
                             reptilian heat.

Trenching the red earth to lay pipe from the new well to the old house. Soon we will no longer need to haul our water in but will have our own spigot to the center of the earth.

September 22   *Javelina and sunflowers.*

Fields of yellow composite flowers flow from across the stream under the fence and up the side of the hill, ending in an ocean of waving wind-swept grasses.

September 23

Expedition through the San Rafael Valley bordering Mexico with Dick Felger, a scientist and teacher of the first order. Visiting Lochiel, the border crossing fifteen miles south of sanctuary where the Spanish conquistadors first entered this country. On to the cold clear waters of Bear Creek, examining each flower and tree, then up over Moctazuma Pass two thousand feet above our oasis home.

September 24

After the long haul to sanctuary and three months of

fine red dust permeating her innards, our Volks bus is exhausted like an old mule. To Tucson tomorrow for a heart transplant.

September 25   *Divine Providence revived.*

I return from rebuilding our engine to find that Tara has come down with a fever, 104.6°. Patricia without transportation or telephone in the wilderness, praying. At noon Joe Quiroga, foreman of the neighboring Mellor horse ranch, responds to Patricia's silent prayers and takes Tara in pickup truck seventeen miles to Sierra Vista doctor. Ear infection; antibiotics. The fever breaks in evening; Tara and Patricia restored to quietude, aching and fatigued.

September 28

A lot of knowledge is being transmitted to us from visitors and friends at the university in Tucson. Experiential realities grow daily as we meet various fellow-creatures here in this remarkable planet salad. Each morning we greet the sun with the Gayatri, the Hindu morning chant:
"OM.
Earth, sky, stars,
Behold the Sun,
Gift of light from the heart of the Source.
May he shape our minds."

September 29   *A V of geese. A cord of oak.*

Thinking today of the story that a well-known wildlife expert told me about arriving to discuss beautiful
bird life with the Lady's Auxiliary to find them sitting
munching chicken. Another conservation-conscious-
ness irony. How many wildlife enthusiasts have a BB
gun or marauding pussycat in the family?

September 30   *A flight of birds near certain*
                      clouds above specific mountains—
                      reality!

Coming back from Nogales shopping, diligent frisk
at the border as per Nixon's hallucination, Operation
Intercept. The beginning of the notorious 'Grass Cur-
tain'. Stopped again by a roadblock at the Sonoita crossroads, thirty-three miles northeast of Nogales. Even the
local ranchers searched at shotgun point. The Man is a
bit too serious for the locals to absolve him of 'fascist
theatrics'; local ranchers angrily finger the 30-30 deer
rifles hung in their pickup cabs. Range war a-brewin'.

OCTOBER

October 1
Nearly full moon, trees silhouetted
in myth. Horses and history.

AUTUMN COMES YELLOW across the grasslands.
The summer rains ended, the surrounding hills
begin again to dry. The cienega, spring, and
stream keep this a green oasis, filled with life and
movement.

Autumn is a time of mountains and wind. There is
a haiku quality to this particular season, each twig distinct as a syllable in tree verse. The sky so full of stars,
blue-black organisms, diamond cellular glitterings, ten
thousand solar systems rising up the spine. A time of
cicadas and drowsy horned toads. Hawks slowly circling. The gathering chatter of birds about to migrate.

The first frost is soon to descend, and with it will
come the dissolution of the insect brotherhood. Cottonwood, willow and walnut drop their deciduous
leaves while juniper and oak remain green, high agave
spines trap the noon sun. The rainbow cactus man-
dalaed just above the ground. Coyotes wail the tribal
song. Fawns charge on strengthening legs. The antlered
buck moves like a phantom through the oak forest.
Javelina string along arroyo bottoms, leaving only their
hoofprints for the morning observer.

Riding the fence experiencing autumn's life I ask
myself who can own another's flesh? Yet we have
bought horses. To own something is to be responsible
for it: to fit into it, finding your place within, your
valence for it, responsible for yourself in it. To own a

horse, to own life, to get upon another's back and tell him where you wish to go. And yet the horse comes to us as it must have to the American Indian—with a change of life style. It opens new experiences, allowing a different approach to wildlings in lonely places; by approaching on another animal one blends better with the natural flow of things instead of permeating the atmosphere with the dragon, man. The horse being a large herbivorous animal has a very gentle emanation, more responsive than a cow yet no more a threat than a deer.

To own a horse, a living creature, is akin to imagining one can own the land, a piece of the living planet; the county clerk is not a holy herald, cannot convey the earth's corpuscles or describe the mineral genealogy of a grazing pronghorn. The Indian knew he could not own the land because he could not control it. Man in his present twentieth century delusion imagines that he can master the land and therefore own it, but it is not so; he and the land erode in constant proportion to the other's lack of native freedom. A horse, like a piece of land, responds in direct proportion to the respect and kindness it is offered. Each willingly offers its energies in response to love.

Patricia had ridden horses much of her teenage life, exercising polo ponies for a friend in her barefoot, orchid-haired Hawaiian childhood. But for me, purchasing a horse was much like planting a garden. I felt a need to tend the well-being of the organism before any sustenance could be requested. I had ridden only a few times in my life, always undisciplined ponies in an undisciplined manner. Now from horseback with

103

a seventy mile visibility, one has a sense of timelessness—or, more specifically, of going back in time to the era when Whitehill settled this land, drawing his timbers of ponderosa pine by horse and oxen fifteen miles down from the slopes of the Huachucas, or a wagonful of saguaro ribs brought up the ten mile trail from the floor of the desert twenty-five hundred feet below—the mountains twenty-five hundred feet above, this land suspended a mile high at the axis of the planet.

The Spanish brought the horse from Spain to Cuba, where great horse ranches were established. Cortez, invading Mexico in 1519, was quoted as saying that horses were his salvation in his victory over the native Indians. It was only twenty years before Francisco Vásquez de Coronado was able to assemble over a thousand head of horses and mules in Mexico for his two year trek up through Sonora in 1540 into what is now Arizona and New Mexico. The scouting parties reached as far as the Grand Canyon. Unable to find the fabled golden city of Quivira, the disillusioned band straggled back. The surviving members of the expedition reached Mexico at last, and Coronado stated, "Next to God we owe our victory to the horses." There was no victory for the Spanish; only the horses seemed to gain more territory, displaying a greater capacity for survival in the environment of the New World than the conquistadors'.

The first real distribution of Spanish horses in what is now the United States came with the founding of San Juan, now Santa Fe, in the upper Rio Grande by Juan Onate in 1598. Mining camps were established and quickly came the need for horses for grinding the ore and threshing the grain, for transportation and for trade. And it was not, as legend has it, by herds of wild horses, once domesticated horses that had escaped, that the Indians came into possession of these creatures. The Indian tribes were traded and sold horses by the Spanish in the seventeenth century. Had they foreseen that this new mobility would allow the Indian to stop the Spanish conquest, the Spanish would never have sold or traded horses to the Indians, as they never would have enslaved the Sobaipuri. This human buffer removed the Apaches swept out of the mountains and drove the Spanish from southern Arizona.

In the years that followed, many horses did escape to the wild, and by 1850 the herds of wild mustangs numbered from five to seven million animals, competing with the cattlemen for the grasslands, water and salt licks. The great Western artist Frederick Remington once wrote, "Of all the monuments the Spaniard left to glorify his reign in America there will be none more worthy than his horse." By the late 1700s horses were plentiful, and Comanche, Kiowa, Apache, Osage, Pawnee, Cheyenne, Arapaho and Sioux were well ensconced in horsedom. The Navahos' trade on the northerly route provided horses to the Paiute and Shoshonee, and even further northwest to the Cayuse, Nez Perce, Crow and Blackfoot, effecting a change not unlike that of the introduction of the automobile—a new technology which required new responses, creating a powerful cultural momentum.

The introduction of the horse changed American Indian society as no ten inventions have affected ours—television, radio, the automobile, the gas stove, and the washing machine together have not caused as radical a change in the consciousness of a people as did the coming of the horse to the life style of the American Indian. And of even greater importance, the horse raised consciousness, not diluted it as the twentieth century extensions of technology may have. The horse was a vision come true, an Element leaked from the Other World, the real world, of which we are only shadows. The horse was integrated into the American Indian's myths and sacred visions in much the same way that Christ entered 'pagan' spiritualism nearly fifteen hundred years before to depict a change in the collective state of mind, an evolution in the Collective Cortex. To know the Plains Indian's culture is to recognize him as a migratory being on horseback, his horseless existence lost in prehistory. His gods were immediately mounted. Whole societies, commerce and religion were based on the trade and mobility of the horse. In fact had the American Indian felt the necessity to record history he might well have dated events BH and AH, Before Horse and After Horse. In the ironic waves and cycles of societies, Wasechu, the white man, brought the Indian to the high point of his culture by introducing the horse before destroying that culture aided by the horse.

So we have bought a quarter horse mare and her one month old filly—Duster a nine year old cow pony raised as a 4H project by one of the Mellors' sons, her filly thrown in like a spare tire. Through Duster we soon came to appreciate the ability and willing strength of the quarter horse, who in colonial times in the tidewater South had come into being by the mixture of Chickasaw Indian mares and English-blooded stallions. We brought her home and watched her lightning mane flowing in the wind as she ran the length of the cienega, a living image of freedom. These gutsy four-square horses, once the backbone of the American cattle industry, are now mostly considered pleasure horses. Yet who has ridden Duster's genetic ancestors in the past? The Spanish vacquero, the Indian, the cowboy; scouts, lawmen, a pony express rider; a circuit-riding parson, an outlaw, or a minstrel. And now this horse, my friend Duster, and I ride slowly the fence, watching bird and beast find their niche away from the eyes of man and horse alike. Her sorrel filly, named Cienega after this rich marsh, frolics behind, passing us, scooting about in circles and back again, freedom beside us as I sit astride the broad back of my horse. But we are called back to the house by our visitor signal, two long toots on Divine Providence to greet the arrival of thirty-five visitors come to see the last of the wildflower display: an orderly brunch on the porch, peeled tomatoes and pickled artichoke hearts, talk, too much talk . . . in late afternoon I escape up to the mesa on Duster at full gallop, yodeling peace cries to the wide sky. And for the first time I experience 'the silver field', the sensory experience of horse and rider as one, our motion interwoven, riding, riding, a centaur at last!

October 4   *A blue ribbon for the dazzling universe.*

On our way to the Santa Cruz County Fair at the Sonoita crossroads we stop at the Mellors' ranch to visit Clint and Cassie; I watch him arrange flowers for the fair while Cassie bakes bread and dry-wipes Mason jars of golden preserves. Clint says, "Here, take these flowers; do something with them." I win first prize for flower arrangement, a large yellow dahlia cactus floating face up with tiny scarlet cactus blossoms between each petal, a sun spinning in a fluid universe.

October 5   *The orioles depart, the marsh hawk arrives.*

Early Sunday morning by the stream, looking at a cross-section of pale green stone, seeking the ancient imprint of dinosaur or grandfather clam—nothing but the ripple flow of rock; no single creature, just fossilized time.

October 13

The last sheet of galvanized metal roofing is hammered into place above Fyodor's scramblings. The end room is reopened, the new adobe hardened and prepared for life in the Southwestern winds. The house finally restored, inhabited by man once again.

October 14   *First frost plates the hills.*

Husks of dead cicada are everywhere—the winter dissolution of the insect people. Ice on the horses' water trough, too thick for soft warm noses; Duster and her filly neigh thirsty frostbreath to the white winter sun.

October 15

We are not as far away from 'civilization' as originally presumed: second Viet Nam Moratorium, a World Village Happening. Synchronicity with a badge: stopped and searched while returning from Sierra Vista, nearest town fifteen miles from sanctuary at the foot of the Huachuca Mountains, as we approach the main gate of Fort Huachuca, the three quarter million acre Strategic Air Command communications center which we are authorized to traverse in our need to reach the neighboring township. But this day we are suspect, in our beards and Volkswagens, and have been singled out to be interrogated for allegiance at the portals of this abandoned frontier fort, now newly rededicated as radar myth center, trigger paradise, where ten years ago roamed a herd of four hundred buffalo shot down from jeeps and halftracks by the new company with M-1s and BARs, festival of the ancient death commemorating the opening of the military lightning center. A barbecue of endangered species by the species which endangers all.

We show the pass which allows us entry to travel this shortcut to the sanctuary. At last the CID and FBI let us through—one separating himself from the others on the sly to tell us that he is really not on 'their' side, flashing a huge brass peace symbol that hung like a plumb bob from his keyring. Must have weighed a pound. And on we go past buffaloes reincarnated as mustachioed twenty-year-olds who flash a V for victory from stockade trucks, gun-guarded beside the road in their military prison uniforms, as we drive through in the gold and blue coveredwagon.

October 16   *Fences checked; deer season coming.*
              Hard frost. Band-tailed pigeons
              hunted in the hills.

The surrounding hillsides have turned rusty cinnamon, the basis no doubt for the name Canelo which in Spanish means cinnamon, these are the Cinnamon Hills. The cienega rises green out of the surrounding autumnal palette. Scarlet flame in the midst of the cienega: an eighty year old pear rootstock gone natural, the pear tree itself long extinct, its healthy root scion grown to full tree ablaze like the autumns I remember from my Northeastern youth. The walnut and fruit trees yellow and fade, the tall grasses become brittle in the northerly breeze. The cicadas are noticeably absent, most insects gone with the coming of winter. The shed skins of snakes. The horses and dogs thicken to the coming cold; for us woolen shirts once again, and the homey feel of fireplace and oncoming winter. The new gas heater blows warm air into a comfortable house as we begin to settle in for our winter work and quiet readings . . . Herman Hesse, Buddhist scrip-

110

tures, Konrad Lorenz. Amazing how each thing corroborates the other. Coyotes bay at the cold moon. The *keerack* of rifles and the dull blast of shotguns outside sanctuary underscore the tune we hum: No Hunting. The band-tailed pigeon flees for its life. Within a week our friends the deer become prey to man's metallic insensitivity. The horses have learned the area well, cross the stream, climb hills—I will begin deer patrol at the end of the month; there will be no slaughter here.

October 18   *Strong winds, the cottonwoods an*
                    ocean full of whales.

In the midst of reading *Demian* I look up to see Tara pushing off from her coffee table roost, taking her first steps. Momma golden retriever singing in the next room, wishing to be let outside to exercise her first heat since the puppies. Life everywhere; even the thick walls of this house do not exclude the ongoing nature of things.

October 19

Family reunion of the Knipe clan by the stream, a rejoicing by the family who offered this land to the Nature Conservancy. The cousins and nieces dance through willow and squaw bush: human joy creating and partaking of sanctuary.

111

October 20

Approaching Tucson rising before us out of the surrounding desert like an ancient cliff dwelling, houses upon houses tight to each other, life packed into the City. In the evening Dane Rudhyar and I read poetry at the Gayatri Bookstore. Then home to an intense downpour, fine droplets of rain in frosty altitude, almost snow. Birdseed in my typewriter again: a poltergeist or Fyodor up to his tricks once more.

October 22   *Heavy frost, hard freeze.*

In the morning mail four colorful Hindu posters from a friend. Centers for the open eye. Shiva meditates in the flickering light of the fireplace. Multi-Brahma Devachan holds lotus darshan at the end of the long pine bedroom. Krishna flutes above the chair in which Patty nurses Tara. Gopi dakinis bless the altar.

October 25   *Very heavy winds, the winter*
pruning. Tara's first word 'hot', the
vocabulary of survival.

Sitting alone before the blazing fireplace for an hour or two before going to sleep, accompanied by a beer, occasionally going out for firewood—eighty year old juniper fence posts as big around as my thigh, pulled from the periphery of the cienega to free her from the constraints of man's 'usage', now freeing solar energy stored since last century to warm us, the homesteader's sun again releasing its heat to warm the homestead house. Looking up into the deeply starred sky, clear night, the moon about to fill, 'three days before, three days after', those six days pinnacled on the full moon, the clearest inner vision and good feeling. The mind likes to watch itself—writing is just a way of talking to myself, of thinking out loud, writing for the joy of it. Searching for a word to describe something hidden in consciousness: the genetic mind, base of the instinctual pyramid out of which consciousness arises, the pulsing of consciousness; Max Planck on a hot tin roof, Leary's molecular consciousness; the consciousness of species, the mind pool, cultural dream pool, the dream beneath which motivates, the underdream, ah yes, that is the word, the *underdream*.

October 27   *Hard frost again; dogs dancing in*
                    silvered grass.

It's eight a.m.; I have been up since six writing. Molten dawn spread over the purple Huachucas. Indian hunting poems speaking through me as counterpoint to deer season coming in a few days. "Ninety thousand hunters loaded and primed for the opening of the season," the Tucson paper says. But this is sanctuary, no hunting; wearing ranger badge on horseback, no hunting; all wildlings left to live, no hunting; take your death wish elsewhere, no hunting. Come stag, fawn, doe; come, whitetail and mule deer, sanctuary.

October 28   27°, the sparrows of winter return.

Dogfight for our bitch's fair endocrines. I try to separate them, remembering Lorenz's wolf as Smith's
hound sinks his teeth into my knee.

October 30   *"And we bring it as sacrifice:*
                              yet there is animal torture
                              and roasting over slow fires.
                              What you are treating are,
                              practically, all problems of
                              cruelty. Are you enjoying it?
                              I tell you in all frankness that
                              I myself have too much of this
                              tragic complex in my body as
                              not to curse it on occasion."

                              Part of a letter to the author
                              from F. Nietzsche via
                              synchronistic Gutenberg.

               I

Today is the day they ship the calves.
From a nearby ranch yipping cowboys
and the bellowhonk of cattle, red
double-trailer stake truck pulled
along side the loading chutes.
Calves separated from cows,
hauled to feed-lot pens, stuffed fat
like Strasbourg geese

114

"four or five pounds a day"
800 pounds to killtime
        5 months away
"highest price yet
38¢ a pound for steer
36¢ for heifers
steer tenderer
heifers fatten quicker . . ."
Inoculated, myacined and drugged
so the fever never comes
until slow eyed death creeps
like a French executioner at dawn
to drag them bawling
        to the adrenalin mists
        of the slaughter house
the groaning butchery to be done
lined up like refugees
        at a bread dole—
the muscled hammer or the sly
pistol right between the eyes
and down they go meat permeated
by dread and shaking,
passed on across the dinner table,
to the grumbling over-
crowded overstuffed denizens
        of the supermarket—
only the well bibbed knife
and fork removing the diner
        from the viking table,
prayerless at the aminoacid
        disintegration

of their fellow beasts—
these broad white-faced cattle
chewed unconsciously by the broad
white face of TV-romantic America.
Swallowed into the dark depths
of the unthought of interior
    taking on the consciousness
    of the animal flesh digested,
the omnivore eating the herbivore
    with table manners,
the Eltonian pyramid in a roasting pan.

II

On the way to mailbox morning
contact with the tribe within
heavy necks of young steer
swing my way,
    pink rimmed eyes
peering between slats
    beside the barn
glassy brown eyes
    into mine
then swing back
    resigned.
The first prayer is recited over their meat
    as I begin to count heads
            then stop
    knowing their lives were bred
            for dying,
        their conception guided
            toward 'the calf crop'.

The ritual cannibalism of the Eucharist
   eating Christ's flesh to absorb his knowing
brought down to octave grass munching,
        herdmind of city . . .
The thought rising
   that when man received his sustenance
   from the silently hunted forest
   the city-pueblo was a planet-hearted community,
        more of the nature
   of the sweet wild beasts
        that supported and religioned life.
The hunter becomes what he hunts,
the butcher the butchered,
the predator the prey—
   each mouthful takes us
   one step further
        from the sun.

                    III

Into evening the mother cows bawling
bulging rebred full of fresh meat
   once again—
Bawling for the calves
hauled out in great red truck
early in the afternoon.
Fat cows bawling full of milk
for sucklings lost to supermarket cellophane
   'best side down'
Bawling
Bawling for the fatted calf
Bawling for the sacrifice

                                117

Bawling to Abraham
Bawling to the innocence of the gopis
Bawling to the blue cowboy, Krishna.

Bawling for the bawling of the herd
Bawling for the pain
   of turgid unsucked teats
Bawling for the chandra-butcher's karma.

Bawling, an intersecting chorus
   of distress;
Bawling to the preternatural light
   of winter coming at 5000 feet
   in the sharply mountained desert.
Bawling . . .
            and the sun sets
                  terrible pink
                  and crimson as slit fish belly.
Bawling . . . setting
   leaving the sky distilled
   to grey light
            dense grey clouds
            holding the coming of winter
            like a cold wet sponge.

            IV

All night an urgency,
a cry to the half moon,
all night cows bawling
in loose groupings,
   one more persistent than the others

between the rancher's house
and the empty loading corral . . .
   sometimes
   just one
      then three or four
  unlike the calling of birds
     an animal cry not
      for territory or mating
   the solemn bellow of suffering,
  like the intermittent sobbing
     at a wake.

Sitting before juniper fire
in the room with saguaro ceiling
thinking it's not a matter of meat
  or meat eating
     it's just the drowsy blindness
     and suffering
     of unnecessary numbers
     of fellow creatures.
And the bellow of our imagined selves.

NOVEMBER

November 1
Deer season opens.
Watchful eyes in the thicket.

L AST EVENING rode the fence at sunset putting up a few more No Hunting signs and checking the gates. It is the first day of deer season, a dozen gunshots echoing off noon; the great Southwestern deer kill is underway. Badged and red-hatted, a red scarf about Duster's neck: poems in the head, eyes on the land. Chanting just below my breath. Have asked the Committee to halt work on the dam as the noise of the dinosaurs scares the deer away, prevents sanctuary.

Two rutting white-tailed stags lock horns in the oak forest just beyond the north fence, oblivious to the distorted mating gestures of man's hunting 'sports'. Their antlers lock now to choose the strongest who will breed with many does, his genes flowing out across the land. These antlers which decide now the future of the species will be shed in February like deciduous leaves to lay on the open grasslands, an added source of calcium for porcupine, rock squirrel, field mouse and packrat. Perhaps even Fyodor rummaging the hillsides has taken back a partially gnawed tine to sequester in his packrat version of Hearst's castle. That man should hunt the deer during its mating season displays his deathly unconsciousness, his absence of vision. A hundred gram lead slug smashing through the skull of a quiet creature browsing on willow twigs and acorns.

If one were to choose to become an animal who could move anywhere in the forest unnoticed and in harmony with his surroundings, one would have to be a deer. A deer preys on no animal though he is preyed on by many. He is trusted by all from the nervous rabbit to the cantankerous rhino. A deer may go where he pleases and though he delights in buttercups, in his wake wildflowers flourish. The center of this animal kingdom in many ways, he is the largest native herbivore and a prime source of flesh to the carnivore life chain. The obliteration markings on deer allow them to blend in with their surroundings almost completely night or day, often making it possible to confuse the cougar's deadly second spring. Of all their predators only man stands taller, the natural white-rumped camouflage becoming a telltale target. And ironically with the passing of the deer's natural predators have passed the natural stamina and health of the deer populations. Although it is estimated that there are more deer now in North America than at the time of Columbus's discovery, the herds are weaker and more given to disease, the slow and malformed no longer pruned from the herd by the natural predator-prey relationship which has guided their evolution. Instead the most beautifully evolved are taken as trophy, the healthiest and strongest removed from the gene pool by a rifle blast.

I hear in the after-echo of gunshots the hunting songs of the Indians who so much revered this land and all its inhabitants. Their hunting chants move through me to demagnetize the spiritual anarchy of Tucson's shiny deer rifles.

I

Hey-ah Hey-ah
One foot follow another
Hey-ah Hey-ah
Come near now
Hey Hey
Close to my bow
Home with me now
Feed us
Hey Hey little deer

Come to me brother deer
Come to me now
Willingly to my
hungry children
to the marriage of quiet death
Through the thick forest
before winter chills you

Deer Deer Deer come to me
so that I may love you
too in death
Come to me as I shall someday come
to the Great Spirit
Hey-ah Hey-ah Hey.

II

I stand very still
I stand very still
Waiting for you

124

Through the forest you move
like silence toward me
I have been standing here
since dawn
waiting for our shadows to collide

I have three arrows
Let one chase your spirit
to the Great Father
Tell him how I love you

I feed my family on your sweet flesh
Tell Him I come in turn

My shoulder stiffens
To your heart all arrow strength—
Go now
Tell Him I won't be long.

November 2

The sun peaks the Huachucas at seven a.m. rolling a
cold front like a glacier before it, gaining in intensity
for several minutes before it fingers the marrow.

November 3   *The hacking guns of the city hunt*
                     the dynamic flesh of the forest.

All about us the echoing rattle of gunfire. A family
of five deer in the meadow, the most we have seen in

125

a single group, grazing unawares. Quince in bloom. Hard frost at night. The white sun of winter rising low across the horizon. New well in, new roof on, fireplace meditations, sweet juniper blaze, Hesse and coyotes, Whitman and willow, hawks and jays, black walnut, wordcycles, earthstories, the planet in motion.

November 4   *Wild asparagus.*

That elusive tribe we speak of seems to be everywhere, faceless, migrating, ever rising into our lives. Could it be that we are reincarnated Indians, balancing the debt? Bringing the planet ledger back into the black. Are these the first planet stewards? A notion rises of something nearly forgotten, nearly remembered, some genetic nibbling at the cortical filmstrip . . .

November 6   *Heavy winds again today.*

Trees shaken loose of their leaves. Cottonwood yellow fans to the earth, a brazen oriental woman.

November 9   *The last kingbird heads south as winter descends on the horizon.*

It is snowing on the steep peaks and canyons of the Huachucas' seven thousand foot rim. The snow-capped peaks dazzling against the clean blue sky.

November 12   *Silver moon crescent, a scythe*
                   cutting toward Antares across the
                   Milky Way. Open heart surgery
                   in the sky.

The planet steward is man working in tune with nature, fulfilling his obligation to the lifespark which animates him. Following an intuitive path indicated by the land the planet steward attempts that sad undertaking of tending injured birds and animals. He does not poison or pollute. In quiet sittings he listens to the land. Planet stewardship is a peace making, a giving away of power and poems. Creating a harmonious nest in the biosphere, the steward imbues a sense of life in his children which sustains them like a healing chant. He seeks neither death penalty nor hunting trophy. He waters the plants and feeds the animals and does not work to waste. For the steward bird song and swaying branch are grace, his meditation a step at a time through the wilderness. His dreams are filled with deer and bobcat, children and trim-coiffed ladies gliding through evergreen boughs. His way is love, his medium is work, his senses are antennae for necessity.

November 13   *Steward plumbing.*

The work continues on the dam to the ironies of man and nature: unexpected rain stopping progress, pumps unsuccessful, breaking down, the backhoe upside down in the creek, one-day rental turned into a week. Have decided to use rock after all instead of ster-

127

ile concrete, planned and replanned; the engineer suggesting rock sturdy enough (done correctly as riprap concrete reinforced formation) to last a 'thousand years'. Now the travail of dozens of trucks hauling rock—but it will be so good to see the cienega secured. There are many places to be protected against the vagaries of man; the Southwest seems immense and unspoilable to the distant viewer, but so did the fragile oceans and the air just a few decades ago. Yellow clouds drift up the valleys from Douglas' smelters sixty miles away. Tucson speaks of 'the smog problem', mountains disappearing in the civilized soup of industry.

November 14   *An early winter drips from the eaves.*

November 16   *Rain into the night. Gray thunderfoot.*

November 18   *12° last night.*

Heavy frost collapses the sedge and marsh grasses of the cienega. Thirty mile winds matting and weaving the flat basketry of the frozen meadow. Early morning frost plates the sanctuary with raw silver.

November 21   *The heavy winds of fall carding the clouds to wisps of raw cotton.*

More than a month until solstice and already winter is here. Temperatures in the twenties the last few nights; freezing winds during midday. My body chapped, wind-blown through wool shirt and levis, microscopic lizard scale along the ribs, evolutionary skin memory. Fire all day in the fireplace, warm hearth beneath a saguaro ceiling. Tara walking in humpty-dumpty Zen slippers on the cold red concrete floor. Winter like a wave of recollection absorbing us in genetic remembrances of the discovery of fire, the burning mandala in the center of the cave: family, wolf poesy rising, Navaho shamanism jingling; always the ongoing vision quest.

Reading some old writings which have come through me: how abstract! And all the time I was Prince Siddhartha, just as confused, before leaving the palaces of the City. Which way to the Bodhi tree?

November 22

Eight a.m. Duster near dead in the stream. For some reason she had entered the creek during the night, stepping into a deep water pocket, moving downstream, ducking a fallen tree and coming up again with her head caught in the fork of a limb, unable to escape. The cold waters numbing her. Lying with her head against the dark mud bank unable to move. Up to my ribs in winter's freezing stream, chain saw like a scalpel so close to her neck, removing the limb. Duster's hind legs hardly able to support her as I coax her further downstream to shallower water and up a gentle bank, then ever so slowly across the cienega toward the corral. Both of us exhausted and numb; barley and the deep warmth of molasses, and good morning.

November 23   *Full moon, last day of*
                                      deer season.

I become extinct like buffalo and bald eagle
Dinosaur was around for 150 million years
Then couldn't make it anymore
I've been here just a million and already
I threaten to take all else with me.

November 24   *To breathe silence, when?*

There is a raven large as a hawk which flies low over the sanctuary early each morning. I have often joined his solitary call. Sparrows rain from the leaf-bare trees into the tall grasses, rising again to the insistence of the dancing dogs.

Sometimes after the machines have stopped their work on the dam for the day I hear silence like a sigh in the oak forest.

November 26   *Thirty mile an hour winds.*

The dam nearly completed. No deer disembodied on sanctuary during hunting season.

November 27   *Thanksgiving blessing—*
                 a celebration of the coincidence
                 of opposites.

The first Thanksgiving
when food was shared
by the Indian and the Pilgrim
was a coming together
of native man and modern man—
the meeting of technology
and our original face.
A feast of friendship.
A feast of convergence.
A feast of the heart.

Let us now, sensing ourselves
in each other, look into our brothers' eyes
recognize the native man
behind our modern masks
and know that we are primitives
of an unknown culture,
the aborigines of the future,
and from us shall evolve
Harmonic Man.
And it is done
we have become
and give Thanksgiving.

November 30

Old Toliver Thudd, the livestock inspector for Santa Cruz County, comes visiting to make sure our horses are hale and hardy, and we spend the day listening to him reminisce about this much-admired part of the county, this last cienega. Bringing too the dire report of rabies everywhere, creeping through the night to infect us; he would make us 'wiser' to the ways of the land, make us fear the unknown as he has since 1909 when he came out in a covered wagon and had to 'fight for every inch of ground', killing each of those 'damn critters' who tried to eat him out of house and home. Explaining to us how reasonable it is to kill each skunk, raccoon, fox, porcupine, coatimundi, rat, each creature who might bite us and give us dreaded rabies. And though dreadful is the disease, the real epidemic is not rabies but a fear of the wild. As we were later to learn, rabies is a natural culling of life forms concentrated in heavier populations than the land can support, the disease spreading through the population, pruning the weakest. Nature's system of checks and balances.

Toliver Thudd tells us stories of foxes smashing through a closed window to attack an unwary housewife nestling her infant in its crib. These beasts! These enemies of man, he says, as he hooks his thumbs in his pockets wise to the ways of killing: the trap, the poison bait, the snare, all his grandchildren safe in their beds while wild sucklings perish in the den, their parents killed for the epidemic hallucination of man.

After supper as Patricia, Tara and I watch the sunset reflected crimson on the Huachucas' western face, across the emerald cienega a white furry creature comes loping toward the house. The hair raises on the back of my neck. A white wolf, I think, bringing rabies across the marsh. Stepping off the porch I approach closer, a machete in my belt, my hand on its handle ready to dispatch this rabid creature. We approach each other, halting, sniffing the air, approaching ever so slowly. And as he comes closer a white flash of fear obliterates the mind and I call out "stop!" and miraculously he stops, dropping down onto his belly. As I move closer he raises up again and moves again toward me, his yellow eyes looking straight into mine. "Stop!" I yell again and he stops and I wonder why indeed do wolves stop when told to do so. Then from over his white rump a white tail goes up like a flag of truce wagging and the Samoyed and I meet. He as relieved as I, an outlaw coming into my arms black with creek bottom mud to mid-chest, a wild dog I suspect but friendly and the communication clear.

Later we discover that he has been brutalized by a nearby rancher who kept him waterless and tethered as punishment for his harmless wandering. More Thudd consciousness torturing the creatures who would find their quiet niche given the opportunity. The next day questioning the neighbor's disregard for the lifestuff of the dog, we explain that now this dog is housed in sanctuary and may stay as long as he wishes. The neighbor grumbles and shuffles off to cowshit barn and the slaughtering of the day. Though *lupus*, bred of wolf, White Guy encompasses us in his wild family and comes home to sanctuary.

December

December 1
A thousand years of history
nourish the grasses.

A FEW HUNDRED FEET east of the stream on the tops of the hills which roll away into oak-studded grama grassland there are traces of the camps and homes of the Sobaipuri Indians, related to the Pimas who presently live in sparse cattledom on reservations throughout southeastern Arizona. The Sobaipuri had many villages along the San Pedro River and Babocomari Creek stretching into this general area. They were a peaceful farming people, raising squash, corn and beans along permanent streams, very much in touch with the land, a buffer between the early Spanish settlers and the Apaches until about the middle of the eighteenth century, dying out slowly from smallpox, the gift of civilization to all primitive peoples, Eskimos and Amazonians alike. Those who survived were rounded up by the Spaniards and forcibly moved to the sites of the Tumacacori and Santa Xavier missions which they built as Christianized slaves, eventually becoming extinct in captivity. When the buffer of the Sobaipuris was removed by Spanish enslavement, their enemies the Apaches swept down out of the mountains and wiped out the Spanish settlements. The Spanish had disturbed the human ecosystem and suffered in much the same way that the planet suffers when we remove the vital links in its evolutionary ecological chain.

The Mexicans tried to ranch in this country and

lasted until the early 1840s, then were chased out also. In the 1830s, word was out that the governors of northern Sonora Mexico were offering bounties for Apache scalps. The Mexicans had become the Apaches' traditional enemies, and were raided often as a convenient source of horses, cattle, and their favorite meat, mules. There even came a time when the Apaches didn't have to hunt any longer but lived instead on captured livestock. When the first Americans came to settle here in southern Arizona, they found abandoned haciendas, ruined irrigation systems, and tens of thousands of wild cattle roaming the countryside.

But the land had changed. Ranchers and homesteaders cut down its trees to build their homes, drained the water table for irrigation, and offered the vast grasslands to the massive overgrazing of their cattle. When in the seventeenth century Father Kino came up through Mexico into what is now O'Donnell Basin, Arizona was a land of great watercourses, shallow lakes, and immense stands of grass as tall as a horse's shoulder. Great beaver dams are described by early explorers and surveyors, an unbelievable lushness surrounding life-supporting waters. At this time beaver were common on every semipermanent stream in Arizona. There was a plenitude of water and enough willow and cottonwood to use for cover. There were probably beaver and otter even in our O'Donnell Creek. But by the turn of the century, after the devastating three year drought of the 1890s most of these plentiful waters had disappeared as had the lush grasslands, and with their demise went the beaver.

When the first Americans came into this country,

the Apaches were not hostile to them. They even offered their services as guides to the army expeditions and settlers who came in with the forty-niners on the southern route across Arizona into California. But among the Mexicans there was still a bounty on every Apache scalp. Whenever the Mexicans came across an Apache village by surprise, they would kill the men and take the women and children to be sold as slaves. The Americans continued to get along well with the Apaches until some scalp hunters invited a band of Apaches to a party on the Gila River and fed the clan poisoned food. After the Indians were dead the bounty hunters cut off their scalps and sold them to the Mexicans. After that the Apaches went to war, and though some clans remained friendly others killed every American they saw. When the Mexican War broke out in 1846 one of the Apache chiefs, Mangas Colorados, one of the most famous chiefs in New Mexico, volunteered his warriors to help fight the Mexicans. But Mangas Colorados too was betrayed by the Americans. By 1860 he had turned against them, and when he came in under a flag of truce to talk peace with his enemies he was captured and tortured, burned with hot branding irons before they cut his head off. The officer in command of Apache territory cleaned the skull and shipped it back to the Smithsonian Institute, where it now sits civilized in a drawer.

The Mexican War of 1846 began another change in this area. Arizona became a highway to the American conquest of California. Although there were no battles here, there were groups of as many as fifteen hundred men coming down the Gila River just seventy-five miles to the north of sanctuary, south of Phoenix. By the middle of the nineteenth century the whole Apache nation was at war with the Americans, and during the Civil War they chased the settlers from the southern valleys of Arizona. It wasn't until the 1870s that anyone dared to resettle and attempt to take possession of the land once again in war with the Apaches. It was at this time, 1878, that Whitehill, the homesteader who settled this piece of land called Sanctuary, built this two-and-a-half foot thick walled adobe fortress against the owners of the land which he now claimed to own. But the Apaches could not be conquered. In this area the Chiricahua Apaches reigned supreme. Just seventeen miles away from the sanctuary—very close to the area now the crossroads at Sonoita, near where Fort Buchanan had been before it was abandoned—the new Fort Crittendon was founded, from which patrols were sent out across the great valley up onto the Empire Ranch and into this area. But their cavalry could not subdue the Apaches until the whites learned to take advantage of the rivalries between various bands and clans. By recruiting members of rival bands as scouts and trackers the army was able to fall on encampments of feuding Apaches and kill as many as could be laid away in the flash of surprise gunfire. It was this disunity which finally dissolved the Apache nation as warriors in the Southwest at the end of the nineteenth century. In the Chiricahua and Cochise Mountains, seventy miles east of us, warriors like Geronimo and Cochise retreated to fight their last fight and surrender without peace.

The land had been tamed, the grizzly and Apache

killed, cattle and Sobaipuri enslaved, the grasslands and watercourses abused, history written in the mummification of the pitted drying earth.

December 7   *Remember Pearl Harbor,*
                               remember Mangas Colorados.

When I was eight years old I wanted to get my third grade sweetheart a Christmas present. With my chin sliding along the yellowing varnish of the dime store 'jewelry' counter I searched through twenty-five-cent treasures, eventually choosing as a token of my esteem a rather large red, white, and blue plaster brooch which stated in script, 'Remember Pearl Harbor'. She was charmed. I was embarrassed. I didn't know who Pearl Harbor was. I bought it because it was the only piece of jewelry which seemed to display any literacy.

December 9   *Birdsong of the inner ear.*

Marsh hawks low across the cienega, a pearl gray adult male and young rufous breasted sailing, hunting, come south for winter from their green Manitoban plains deep with high country snow. A torn rabbit beside the corral is another mark of survival. Red-tailed hawks in that odd white phase sitting like owls on a craggy oak. The turkey vulture gone until March. The rough-legged hawk arrived south for the winter. Ravens careening, chased by sparrowhawks from their ridge. By the new dam the smaller birds shelter in the skeletons of cottonwoods and currants. Bluebird, nuthatch, sparrows, and the beloved brown towhee who watches himself in the tractor's rearview mirror like a TV performer before a studio monitor. The squawk of the belted kingfisher.

December 14   *Lunch beside the alligator-barked*
               juniper, an acorn woodpecker for
               company, a raven overhead
               surveying our sandwiches.

Letter from a friend today about his trip through the South Seas, following those first travelers who became the American Indian. From volcanic Polynesian paradise past the islands of Japan up through the Aleutians and down into the wintry heart of North America, clockwise, against the sun, toward new fires of beginning. And on to Oraibi, about two hundred miles north of us, where blossomed the four migrations that peopled this continent before returning again to their Oraibi mesa home . . . Are we primitives of an unknown civilization, or unknowns of a primitive civilization?

December 17   *The straight-backed silhouette of*
               ducks against the purple
               sunrise sky.

Immigrants, a ragged flight avoiding duck season, descend in slow parabola across the hills into the thick

141

grasses that encompass the spring. The year is nearly
over and a new hunting season has just begun.

December 20   *Bluebird synchronicity.*

By the stream I notice the first arrival of the eastern
bluebird: fat blue back and wings, thick rufous breast,
quick tail. Returning to the house to tell Lady Patricia
of my find, to be greeted with her own announcement
of their arrival.

December 21   *A poem begun long ago, too soon.*

First snow falling
air moving white
through bare branches
across wind-woven basketry
of frosted cienega sedge.

Waking this morning
to reborn high savannah
   white mountains below gray sky
   teeth of gaping valley jaw,
   snow arroyo.

Waking this morning
to eleven pups born
during the night
to the silent slant of snow—

each crystal perfect
the lacy fossil
of some forgotten organism.

Leather-leafed arthritic oaks,
cottonwoods leafless, hibernating:
snow pelt over pitted bark
flowing southerly to the Mexican tundra
moss northerly to the Arctic.

Bird leaf branch fluttering
replacing shed autumn
masked sparrows and redcapped finches
the breasts of bluebirds glowing
like a potbellied stove,
the acorn woodpecker's constant calculations
warbler snowsong—
each leaf evolved to lizard scale
evolved to feather.

A marsh hawk over frozen grass
by the glistening spring.

Snow falling
from Christmas heaven
crystals
    crystals
        crystals.
Snow-form falling
from vapour heaven,
its opposite in steam
imagined from a kettle.

The pups whirring
to mother's ample belly.

Snow mind gliding back
eleven years to the sixth floor window
of the New York State Psychiatric Institute—
a dozen of us sitting and standing,
two nurses also,
grouped about that recalled window
watching first snow fall
on thick swan-necked Hudson.

    Street lights frame
    the soundless slant of snow
    cowled above in white
    snow monks on a silent vigil.

Each of us watching
snow slide to city-planet
very still in dark rec-room
silhouetted by city lights below.

All silent watching
snow unbroken
on Riverside Drive.
Twelve silent victims
of the concept of madness
watching
lone car rip
long tire-tread
    lizard scale
through the unbroken white.

144

Tears in every eye
the nurses' too
a soft sob
joining us all
in the primal sense of innocence lost
and our tragic rescue from Paradise.

Each quietly back
to his room,
the snow nurses buried
in the fluorescent anti-snow
of the dispensary.

Later lying in bed
watching snow slant
past window
the mind's steam condensed
to that first poem
whistling through my head
in astounding cadence,
teakettle of the skaldic mead—
the mind a footnote to Eliot's Wasteland.
Verlaine assassinating me
around every corner
Mayakovsky and Rimbaud bobbing
like corks on a net
cast into the opening sea of intuition.

The huddled coo of pigeons
pacing on a nearby ledge.

Sleep—

the earliest dreams of poetry
written in snow—
Haiku handprint
in a heaving drift.

Evicted from the madhouse
one month later.
Born again to life
on New Year's Eve
suitcase in hand
alone into a white world
ripped by tires—
those first poems
in my winter pocket,
perfect, each line
repairing the snow.

And from then to now
  11 years through the first snows
  of the mind
  in a poem on a pine table
  in the room with saguaro ceiling
snow falling,
          skywindow.

December 25

Christmas morning begins beside blazing juniper
fire, presents spread like fallen acorns across the floor,
yearling Tara entranced as much with the wrappings
as the contents: a wooden horse, a table and chair set,

146

warm winter clothes, crayons and bubbles. Patricia in her Santa Domingo Indian turquoise and silver necklace, healing beads containing the mineral history of the Southwest, reflecting the blue sky and the glint of frost etched on the window panes. My present a pair of 8x50 wide-angle binoculars to allow closer inspection of the life we wish not to disturb. A new dimension of our interaction with the wildlings roosting in the snow draped streamside woodlands.

In the afternoon the visitors for the party begin to arrive. Local ranchers and cowhands join long-haired friends from Tucson and the neighboring Shri Ram Ashram to celebrate the birth of the Christ of us all. A world of different realities intersecting, the clans brought together in a ceremony of open communication; neighboring cultures dissolved in a glass of hot spiced wine. Each chat beginning from the soles of the feet, land the common frame of reference for vegetarian and cattleman alike. A common preference for wilderness, rather than for altering life to suit us; agreement and benediction across the thousands of acres which separate and join us all. Sanctuary for man as well. Rock musician and truck driver, cowboy and yogi, horseman and painter, planet stewards all at this moment of the cross.

December 31   *Snow.*

End of the year. End of the decade. Reborn twice in these ten years. Mountains rise and fall. New Year's Eve, very much at home in snow winter pocket of planet.

147

JANUARY

January 1
Winter is a time of sparrows and hawks.
The great and subtle clear as frost on lichen.

AT FIRST the names of birds carried a strange and even jocular sound to my ear: goatsucker, kittiwake, ferruginous hawk, flamulated screech owl, clatter rail, scaup. A rufous-sided towhee sounded like a World War I fighter plane. Then I came to recognize in the sounds of birds' names a mantric quality, chantlike, an intonation which invokes the freedom of flight and the organic. At last I heard in the names of birds their song. Birds sing in response to inner states, as involuntary and natural an expression of mood as a happy man humming or a sad man sobbing. Often, too, birdsong is the expression of the mood of the flock in much the same way that humans' laughter or sadness is carried on through the group, an emotional contagion which signals states of mind. Then the sounds became clearer: great blue heron, varied thrush, phainopeplia, ruby throat, night hawk, rough-winged swallow, purple martin, meadow lark, merganser, grebe, cormorant, chickadee, avocet, lazuli bunting. Each sound emanating like the wind through the trees, a species of its own. Each sound transmitting a mood in color and form. As it is said in the ancient Upanishads, the energy of the One is divided into the forms of the ten thousand, and here we see it reflected in the myriad shapes and colors of birds. Like a single shaft of light refracted through a prism, each species takes separate form in sound: whimbril, sanderling, marbled

150

godwit, crossbill, roadrunner. Each creature taking on an aspect of the universal, each winged being taking flight like a thought grown to a state of mind finding its niche in the greater mind manifest as planet. Plover, petrel, stint, solitaire, dove, olivaceous flycatcher, arctic warbler, cactus wren, acorn woodpecker, yellow-shafted flicker, anhinga, cedar waxwing, weaver finch, widgeon. Each state of mind a bird with its particular reality.

Of all wildlings, except of course for the insect brotherhood, birds are the most often seen. They exist everywhere, from the antarctic to the North Pole. They vary in color as much as flowers, and for much the same reasons. Birds, like humans but few other warm-blooded creatures, are visually oriented. And what's more they sing. Not far from the heart, the syrinx stretches the breath of life to form life's song. Their chants reach us everywhere. In the city their flights raise our eyes from the pavement. In the suburbs many find a harmony with man: the cedar waxwing beneath a berry-filled pyracantha, drunk by the back door; sparrows quarreling at a feeder; a barrage of juncos from the oaks into the flower garden; the ever-present jay policing the bird population; a sparrow hawk following a car down a back road, sampling insects the car chases from the roadside grassland; the mockingbird singing through the night to lighten our dreams; the grackle and the blackbird meeting on a golf course to discuss the world of feathered forms; the robin prospecting in the back yard, serenading man as he lies in bed conjuring the coming day. And as the world climate changes these feathered minstrels extend their range so that each year we see more and different species which somehow survive the home gardener's pesticides and the developers' million-acre-a-year habitat destruction, though eagle, condor, pelican, prairie chicken, passenger pigeon, and others succumb to man's predatory life style. Across the sky which shelters us all, geese and ducks; on the seashore gulls, sandpipers, herons and coots grace our life with their individuality. Birds display possession without ownership or murder; they teach us song and architecture, dance and how to fly.

January 2

An inexplicable green glow from beyond the ridge lights the night sky. Ten degrees at midnight; freezing winds during the day. Nuthatches and indigo buntings, ruffled to the cold, sit like dried fruit in the bare apple tree. The marsh hawk sailing back and forth across the cienega like a pendulum locks us in terrestrial time as counterbalance to the extraterrestrial glow that fossilizes the night sky.

January 5   '*Neither sleet nor rain nor dark of night, etc.*'

The US Mail's motto of man against nature. Yet often it works and we are in touch with old friends and the past.

152

January 8   *Mexican jays ousted from the*
                             cottonwoods by kamikaze
                             woodpeckers.

January 9   *A quick change in temperature,*
                             clear days and nights without
                             frost.

In Tucson, 70°: the nation's high. The horses sweating, furred to winter. The moist soils of the cienega warming beneath a thick woven grass mat. And as a friend was told, speaking with old-timers in an eleven state migration west of the Rockies, "There is no more average weather, son. Snows in May, bone dry in winter, no water for irrigatin', then when it does rain it spots the crops. There's less pollen and less honey and the matin' season's shorter. No more average weather dammit, can't count on anything but change!"

January 10

Phainopeplia (the silky flycatcher) shimmering black, an abbot in the apple tree. Three acorn woodpeckers dart from a hole in the family cottonwood flying precise acrobatics like a daredevil stunt squadron. Bluebirds, indigo against dull green of Mexican blue oak.

January 11   *Frost replaces the sun.*

153

Red-capped male house finch among lady finches in the oak before the window. A ready response to yesterday's bird seed. A beautiful young rufous sparrow hawk, tail flicking on dry apple twig branch. Dead manzanita twisted about yellow and orange lichened rocks like driftwood thrown to the shore.

Two immense gray tree squirrels, high in an Arizona black walnut.

A young gila woodpecker stopping over in mulberry tree, then off to Mexico.

January 14   *Silver-edged sparrows in morning sun. Doves in quince. Easter bluebirds in pear trees.*

In my silent sittings I am often reminded of the infinitesimal part we each play in the composition of the cosmos. The concept of planet stewardship, of such great importance to me as I sit in the heart of this frost-gilded sanctuary, seems almost lost in the constant depletion of the planet's natural beauty. But then I recall a postscript to a letter from an English poet friend which stated, "I suspect we shall succeed before most are aware we exist." And I roost a bit easier.

January 16   *Good news for the planet.*

A hundred miles north of us fifteen thousand acres of remarkable Ara Vipa Canyon has been secured by the Nature Conservancy for eventual transfer to the

Defenders of Wildlife. A huge refuge for innumerable wildlife species existing in pristine natural balance has been preserved to allow the continuance of this unique area. Ara Vipa Creek causes a luxurious growth of desert flowering plants, shrubs, trees and cacti to emerge from the harsh Sonoran desert of southern Arizona. Like the stream which runs through our sanctuary, Ara Vipa Creek rises in the pine forests of a nearby mountain range flowing underground until it bursts to the surface in the desert twisting and turning for twenty miles through the narrow canyon. This biologically special place is home ground for eagle, mountain lion, rattler, two rare and endangered species of fish, the gray hawk, the rare zone-tailed hawk, and northern black hawk, and the only known maternity colony of the Mexican leaf-eared bat. Nesting high on the sheer volcanic cliffs that overlook the stream are the golden eagle and the Mexican black hawk. About the deep desert stream congregate a variety of life forms which coexist in no other area.

Our sixty acres is relatively small, at best a thought-form, an alternate lifestyle offered in harmony with the planet—an antenna for healing, a greeting to the stars. That is why we feel so close to each act of stewardship, such as building the dam to preserve the oasis or removing the fence posts from the cienega to allow the wind unbroken movement across this precious breeding ground. Our neighbors seem to have changed somewhat: less hunting it appears, and a greater concern for injured wildlings; often they have brought us the starving and the broken winged. Our personal interchange with advancing young biologists from the

University has been fruitful, our ethic of what 'collecting' really amounts to exchanged for the scientific microscopic view of the planet and all life thereon. Few of these students really want to kill; equally few realize that collecting specimens is killing. We are still trying not to be self-righteous, trying to listen. When do they start conveying wisdom instead of knowledge at the universities? It can be conveyed by induction, at least, if an adequate model is made available. Perhaps someday planet stewardship will be a required course. That we have to eat the planet is a fact of life; sticking a pin through it or putting it in a killjar is a treacherous trick of the mind, a misdirection gone to excess, like not learning from previous wars. We can learn from those whose work has come before; ten thousand new animal- or bird-skins for a collection is just more drowsy blindness.

Talking last week with a young couple, biology graduate students, I mentioned that I had seen a brown thrasher earlier that day. "Gee, I sure would have liked to shoot that!" he exploded. "With a camera or a gun?" I asked. "Either way," he said; "don't have one in our collection at the University." And all I could think of saying was, "If we kill the ones we seldom see we'll never see them again." And yet there is a joy in even this sort of exchange, a realization of having gone beyond the insensate environment in which we have all been programmed.

January 19

Approaching the front gate, a little sharp-shinned hawk on the fence post eyeing the many smaller birds which comprise his diet. Down from Canada, this small edition of the Cooper's hawk spends his winter at sanctuary scanning the sparrow-filled field. I watch him rise from the post, spiraling upward, hardly flapping his wings. Through my binoculars he angles higher and higher on a rising thermal until nearly out of sight. Then, directly over a line of trees he dives like a fighter plane, his wings half folded against his body, straight down a thousand feet into the top of one of the giant cottonwoods, then out again, a sparrow caught in his steel sharp talons. Back to the fence post he finishes his meal as each creature continues its song to the natural rise and fall of things.

January 21

Deer track in my sleep last night, 'bird's foot alluvium wash'; mother sea mating with the beach. A wet dream.

January 26   Poets honing the clouds.

Jose Arguelles arrives from California to spend a few days re-energizing us with his concept of organic revolution. The true revolutionary, he says, is a seed of the new and in being a seed he fulfills the purpose of all life; one more re-volution of the life cycle. Going from one level of the will to another. The most thorough revolutionary is by nature an alchemist, he says, understanding that change is part of the process of further evolutionary initiation.

In the midst of this serious mentation Jose yelps as a black ant bites him on the ass. "We learn our lessons," he said, "from, and in, the strangest places."

January 28   *Jose departs like a dove.*

January 31   *Cold and clear.*

Seeking light between the tides of the mind like a shore bird scampering before incoming waves, culling microscopic sustenance.

FEBRUARY

February 1
Cattle vs. unreal estate.
Man vs. illusion.

L ESS THAN A MILE AWAY is the Ewing's Triangle Z
Ranch through which we must pass to reach the
gate that opens onto sanctuary. Bud and Margo
Ewing, deep listening, soft eyed folks come to Arizona
for the peace in the eye of the storm which is this
world. During the second World War, working in the
Philippines, captured by the Japanese as the imperial
white-eyed enemy; corralled in a concentration camp
for the duration. Returned to their native land raising
cattle and fine horses they now expand with the horizon, nested in the wide open spaces that counteract the
claustrophobic visions of the past. As though we were
expected we have been greeted by our neighbors who
through a chain of coincidences welcome us as friends.
Margo, raised in Hawaii, an alumnus of the same
school which Patricia attended in Honolulu; Bud born
and raised in Mill Valley, California, our stomping
ground for the last five years. With their warm greet-
ings we took our place within the ecosystem like burrowing owls who assume residence in the den of another, joining an already established community.

The cattle industry in the Southwest is dying. Bud,
trusted by all has taken on the presidency of the bank
in Patagonia. Open three days a week, four hours a
day, an old western style bank of stucco and wrought
iron, the outlaw hordes not far away. The short grass
prairies are drying, the cost of feed has risen drastically

and with water becoming scarcer fewer cattle can survive on the range without supplementary nutrition and complicated watering systems.

The cattle industry is moving to the old plantations of Georgia and the Southeast, cattle replacing the slaves, continuing the precedence. The diminishing return of cow punching in the Southwest has come during a period when land has increased in value, and so the ranches are sold to developers, miners and sportsmen to do what they will with what remains. The value of the range increases in direct proportion to the expansion of the human herd, seeking wilder paradises, a second home on the land too easily tamed. Those bestial cattle removed from the range, seen only through cellophane in the supermarket. Just as some locals think that sanctuary or any piece of land is wasted if not used for cattle, the grass turned to flesh, the flesh turned to cash, so it is felt by others that the ranges themselves are now too valuable for the cattle. Reversing transcendence, the black alchemist of technology turns gold to dross. The earth altered by landscaping and modern times introduced by the men who seek tighter housing on the cliffs of the world. Where it was the alchemist's dedication to take what was less and make it greater, the black alchemist developer takes the gold, the pure land, and turns it to dross, the impure human-eyed clutter of inhumane housing. And what an odd term 'developer' is, as he does not develop but instead destroys what has developed through a billion years of evolution. As an Arizona legislator said about the movement to preserve wilderness, "A golf course is all the ecology I care to know about. The eighteenth hole is as much nature as I can stand."

So the cattle industry moves from the Southwest, its first great cradle on this continent, the cattlemen prodded and cajoled by realtors like the cattle themselves for what can be made of the meat of the earth. Grass once sold to the butcher as calf is butchered on the spot, sectioned and gouged by Caterpillar tractors. And caterpillar is a proper designation for that blight which gnaws its way across the earth, breaking the ancient humus to reach the sterile clay into which foundations are pounded. The earth is sold as though real estate were something real and could be possessed, but indeed it is unreal estate, merely the concept of ownership which is sold.

The cattle have eaten themselves out of house and home and in so doing have affected the lives of all about them. The range is left ridged with cattle paths and stripped of grass cover, removing much of the natural browse of deer, forcing them to eat the bark of shrubs otherwise saved for their winter sustenance. In the cold of winter the deer are found starving in the hills. Black-tailed deer accompanying the drying trend uphill replace the native whitetail, the semi-arid country more suited to their desert life style. The whitetail retreat into the Huachucas replaced as subtly as the oaks by the cyclical change of nature and the human cycles which have allowed overgrazing of the land.

But the stripping away of grass cover affects more than the large herbivores, more than the cattle or deer.

The greatest enemy of the increasingly rare Mearns quail is the cow. Oxalis, a small plant whose tubers the quail depend on, has been rooted out by cattle, greatly reducing the food supply which once supported large bevies. Good grass cover is essential to the survival of the Mearns, protecting it from predators, hidden from the swoop of the Cooper's hawk and the pounce of the bobcat. And in destroying their own habitat as would no other animal in a natural balance with his environment, the cattle have destroyed the environment for deer and quail, prairie dog and fox, burrowing owl and black-footed ferret, beaver and river otter.

With man's antibiotics and artificial survival mechanisms the cattle have multiplied as no natural population would on the range, and now they have no place to go but to feedlots and richer lands. And the cattlemen have no place to go but to the city. Or perhaps remaining on an acre or two of a once large ranch, the cattleman watches trucks and bulldozers carve the land into tracts for the cattlelike housing of the developer.

Telling us of this trend in the Southwest, having increasingly been absorbed into sanctuary by conversations about drainage and water conservation, Bud and Margo Ewing have decided to protect the southern end of the cienega which extends onto their property. And the Ewings negotiate with the Nature Conservancy to tear down the fences between cattledom and sanctuary, to encompass the whole cienega in a refuge, returning to the planet what remains of its natural heritage.

Gray-brown hunchbacks dragging crumbs back to the monastery. Another foray on the playpen at the other end of the bedroom which houses the horned lark we found last week by the roadside suffering from insecticide poisoning. Now, after multiple doses of activated charcoal and milk 'Horney' is cured, though sufficient damage has occurred to render him flightless. Luckily, being a ground bird he is not too despondent at the loss of flight, momentarily as content in his three-foot-by-three-foot pen as he would be on the ground. But he is deprived of that rapturous spiraling flight of the nesting season in which he circles nearly out of view, hovering on fluttering wings to project his incredible love song. These horned larks, their black horn-like tufts rising from pinkish cinnamon heads, have been our constant companions on our rides through the brown grasslands of the surrounding desert plains and hills, often hopping fearlessly on ahead of us. Occasionally we see them in days of intense desert heat standing in rows in the shade of fence posts and sacaton grass with mouths open, panting. Now at home with us, Horney's song fills the morning hours as the sun falls through the window warming part of his enclosure. The seed from his bowl scattered across a wide area of his 'ground'; at night sharing his food with the other inhabitants of the house, the mice he knows so well from the grassland to which he may never return.

February 7   OM's Law:
                    what ever goes up must.

   Mescalito and I walk the stream toward the sun, sitting, watching moss become forest, become planet,
become stars, become moss. Zen garden on the back of
a turtle. Then return to an overstuffed chair in the
house, the energy somehow draining from my body.
An hour in the chair unable to move, then with great
effort ever so slowly outside to flop down on the bare
earth, feeling very old. An awkward suspicion rising
that somehow my vital forces were absorbed by the
thick adobe walls. Is it low blood sugar, or history sunk
deep within the ancient house? Thoughts of the four
year old Indian girl's skeleton found in a shallow grave
a few hundred feet from the house. And always that
subtle 'presence' of the Old Indian. Not ghosts but
guests . . . Later resurrected by coffee, the earth replacing my energies: the stars poking through the blue-
black sky, the physical body reinforced by the energies
of my subtler form.

February 13

   On a platform of sticks high in leafless black walnut,
a huge porcupine, mate perhaps of the dead male found
last summer still clutching a broken limb, shot through
the head before this became sanctuary. Parent perhaps
of the two younger porkies found dead nearby. Mother
mourns man in the treetops.

February 14

Gila woodpecker stabbing at a dried pear, bobbing like a Christmas ornament at the tip of a winter branch.

February 15   *House finch in the manzanita behind the house.*

So this is the morning tenor I had been unable to identify. In honor of his fanciful song and bright red chest I wear my orange turtleneck today.

February 17   *Spring creeps on its elbows into sanctuary.*

Willow near budding, the cottonwoods' yellow catkins dangling like miniature beehives, humming with yellow bees arriving everywhere at once. Almost seems as though the bees emerge from the flowers as they open. Pollen floating on the clear creek. So often on the land one is made aware of the perfect synchronicity of things, how one thing accompanies another in what seems the same moment. Multidimensional choreography.

February 18   *An everyday occurrence from the porch.*

Phoebe dawnsong. Bluebirds. House finch singing to

gray-headed junco. Marsh hawk low across the cienega. A family of woodpeckers copping acorns from an ancient limb. Chipping sparrows, mourning doves, ravens. The golden eagle slow and powerful above a red-tailed hawk. Mexican jays, sparrow hawk. A mummified empty-socketed gopher snake still coiled in hibernation, probably found by jays in a niche of the old well.

February 22

Sun over red-streaked mountains. Winter melting gold in the marsh; the stream clear and cold.

And now it is javelina hunting time, pig season. Our stewardship of the sanctuary can almost be divided into man's predatory seasons: dove season, deer season, duck season, band-tailed pigeon season, quail season, javelina season and year-round open season on those wildlings designated as varmints: skunk, fox, porcupine, bobcat, badger, raccoon, civet, ringtail, coatimundi; and the glory targets: jaguar, mountain lion and bear, all huntable without necessity of permit, each considered a danger to man's domination of the land. Today to shoot the bristly pig is all they want, but to slay the shiny-haired pig of ourselves, when shall we find that insightful weapon?

February 23   *The last meditation of winter,*
a formula from the fire.

Sitting before the fire
    alone and surrounded,
    Apaches just eighty years behind
    that manzanita.
Watching my original face
    evolving in the flames
the fire's reflection
    exploring the walls of the cave
beyond the dark window
mountains beneath a dark sky
and a feeling
    that I am only here
    to record it
archetype of myself
    before the fire
    returned to sanctuary.

February 24   The first lightning of spring,
                   thunder over dark mountains, the
                   sky reflecting the earth in clouds
                   building mountains
                   over mountains.

   Been here eight months today and the demagnetization has just now truly come about. I am considerably
more active now than before but somehow less at-
tached to what I am doing. Attempting to practice aus-
terity in speech, honest and beneficial (a hard act to
follow); yoga flowing like a microbe back from extinction into the bloodstream, a strengthening bacterium
which helps digest reality.

170

February 25   *Stopping at a pool of thought.*

Large gray fish with white underbelly in catchpool downstream. The wing of a dragonfly protruding from his mouth, a ferocious flick of his tail breaking into saber tooth and lightning, food chain trailing in his wake. Molecules of insect flesh returned to the muddy bottom where the scavenger Catostomus waits patient as evolution.

February 26   *Cold nights remembering snows of late December. Clear skies, the sun yellows to spring.*

Patricia and Tara, giggling yearlings in pillow land. Tara climbing, reaching, rattling, gabbling, stumbling, jumping, laughing, a year and a half into it.

February 27   *Meetings with remarkable men.*

Rudhyar comes to visit, lunch and lawn chairs in the sun. A nuthatch in an oak beside us, listening to our every word, foraging between our syllables like picking insects from furrows in the bark; then off after a butterfly.

171

A zone-tailed hawk
a great horned owl
two coyote
a fox—
carcasses hung
on a barbed wire fence.

The farmer's field protected
the horseman's pasture protected
the rancher's range protected.

The hawk's outstretched wings
entwined in crucifixion;
the owl's great head
brushing the earth
his fiery talons toward
the hollow sky;
the thin coyotes grimace,
teeth bared, blood frozen
in the desert sun.

The gray fox draped
on the fence post
like M'Lady's wrap—
a First Nighter
at Death's round table.

The earth protected from grace,
locked in human time—
ruined bodies on a barbed wire fence.

MARCH

March 1
Spring in the lowland desert.
A visit with the cuckoo people.

DRIVING THE BACK ROADS around Tucson I pull
the bus onto the lowland desert to watch a
roadrunner dart out of the brush and race
down a path at breakneck speed before disappearing in
the dense chaparral and cactus of his homeland. Tara
emits a high frequency pitch of glee as he throws his
tail over his back and ducks into an immense mass of
sticks and trash under the lower branches of a mesquite. In the middle of the trampled depression which
serves as a nest is a lining of snakeskins, feathers and a
stolen diaper probably gleaned in roadside refuse
collecting.

The whimsical roadrunner, symbol of speed and
cunning, adopted by Detroit as an image of agility,
streaks past like a brown and white feathered ava-
lanche, becoming bronzy green as the tail disappears
once again in his incessant hunt for food. A large black
cricket disappearing down his long thick bill to the
waggle of his bristle-tipped topknot crest. The yellow
ring about his eyes emphasizes the stiff eyelashes which
personalize his face. He is the shabby desert scavenger,
ridding the desert of many of the creatures man in his
self-defensiveness considers pests—crickets, caterpil-
lars, beetles, centipedes, mice, lizards and other reptiles, including horned toads and his favorite delicacy,
the fire-eyed rattlesnake. His incredible ability to ma-
neuver, leaping and divebombing to deliver stab after

stab at the base of a rattler's skull, makes him a most welcome friend to those living in the saguaro forests or cholla foothills. Many legends have grown up about this disheveled whirlwind of energy and agility, especially those tales relating his two- and three-hour battles with large rattlers. In our first week at the sanctuary we were told stories by our neighbors and the workmen on the dam of the cunning of roadrunners working in teams to worry and subdue the tasty desert rattlesnake. One of the workmen told us of watching two roadrunners attacking a poised six-and-a-half-foot diamondback rattler, his fourteen node rattle shaking in war tremor to warn disaster to that which might approach. One roadrunner fixed the swinging gaze of the rattler while the other with rapier beak attempted to find that point at the back of his skull where the energy of the spine opens like a fountain into the brain. To sever that junction is the roadrunner's culinary art. These two roadrunners attacked again and again to little avail, until at last one of them disappeared to return with a segment of round thorny cholla. Piece by piece, coming and going while the first roadrunner, just out of striking distance kept the rattler on the defensive, the other roadrunner encircled the rattler with a thorny fence of spiny cholla segments, literally capturing him so the final coup de grace could be struck at their own pace, at their chosen moment when the rattler's attention was drawn away just long enough from the fierce charge of the second roadrunner. Then followed a three hour feast, the rattler disappearing an inch at a time down the epicurean esophagus.

March 3

A year ago today, two months before we met Huey
Johnson, the Knipe clan congregated to decide what
was to become of the family homestead empty for years
since Grandma Knipe, called Granno, had passed on.
For three decades Grandma had lived alone in the old
house. The neighbors, a bit peeved that their social expansion had been retarded, said she was 'eccentric'.
But Granno just didn't want people on the land, "it
disturbs the animals." She had felt the spirit of the
land, speaking to the ancient chiefs long since passed
from the hills or the deer eating from her wrinkled
palm the native grains and fresh sweet corn she grew
for them alone. She had found her place watching
skunks dance in a circle in the moonlight, talking to
the old brown bear or winking at the bobcat scuttling
into his rocky den beneath the spreading roots of the
great oak beyond the stream, more afraid of the sun
than Granno's good morning salute. It was Granno
who had drawn throughout the house the symbol designs of the Hohokam, the canal-building agricultural
Indians of eight hundred years before who first cultivated this land and left it whole for their descendants,
the Pueblo and Papago. Hohokam frescoes along either
side of the fireplace direct the smoke toward heaven.
On the weathered exterior wall of the porch she had
incised in a mandala the lizard and lightning signs of
the Hohokam's integration of earth and heaven.

Granno's presence is everywhere, particularly about
the house where she spent her last thirty years watching the seasons and speaking with the animals. It was

178

Granno who first consecrated this land, it was her attitude which was the predecessor of sanctuary.

March 7   *Mousefoot in dream ear.*

Woke suddenly to white foot of mouse in my ear, he as surprised as I. Must have gotten lost on his way to the horned lark's playpen. Don't mind them scurrying across the floor or even stashing their seeds in my underwear and socks, but he'll have to explore for the Northwest Passage elsewhere.

March 10   *First vermilion flycatcher by the stream. Red-shafted flicker. Meadow lark cienega song.*

Communication through the window to our injured friend healing in the sun, nesting on a piece of soggy whole wheat bread.

A busload of visitors from a local Audubon Society come to see the beginning of spring in the high Sonoran life-zone. Clouds over cinnamon mountains. The migratory birds have begun to arrive. The first warblers congregate in a leafless mesquite overseen by the resident sparrow hawk ensconced atop the Chinese date tree. Chipping sparrows pour down from the cottonwoods, and too our little comrades the mosquitos reappear, partaking of our flesh. Cold at night, but mostly sunny days; feels like I've been here always, and, as Lew said, there is nowhere else we need to go.

March 15   *Spring resurrection.*

Succulent green shoots break through last year's
golden grama stubble. The hillsides flower once again.
The palette replenished.

March 19

Serving the steward's apprenticeship to the planet.
Learning out loud in this journal of days and species.
Daily meetings with new plants and animals, birds and
insects, reptiles and outcroppings, constantly renew
insight into the interdependent continuum. "The use
of the useless," Chuang Tzu said. No weeds, just the
inescapable order of a perfect wild garden, each individual coming forth and passing back in its time. To
serve the planet for its own sake. To wait patiently as
an oak for spring and dance the dance of the great
liberation.

March 21   *Vernal equinox.*

Here spring is willow bud, stream-flow of native fish-
form. Turtles. Asparagus in warm soil, wild. Migrations.
Ducks north overhead, randomly strung between
clouds. The horned larks have departed, except for
the one singing in the bedroom. The turkey vulture
and the vermilion flycatcher have arrived. The ghosts
of buffalo graze on the undergreen of hills. Porcupine
out of spidery leafless walnut skeleton. Javelina like

a string of geese across the hill. Deer and coyote. Jaguar in the Sierra Madre. A black bear relocated by neighboring ranchers, both wiser than before. Apricot redbuds, apple blossoms; Jimson greens first, lobelia just beneath the soil. The badger by the stream seeks a new home. And it's time to begin spring planting, Buddha beard and hoe in mind's hand.

March 25

As guide to the sanctuary the best I can do is be an usher accompanying each spectator to the species of his greatest interest. Ornithologists I take to see the small green heron or the painted redstart. Reptilian biologists I introduce to the rare rock rattler or the disappearing tail of a Sonoran whip snake, or perhaps indicate with passing pat on the head a puppy-like horned toad along the path. With ichthyologists lazy by the stream, watching dace knit shadows to the shore as my friend catostomus plows the dark depths. Or with a geologist walking the bottom of the deep arroyo, walls rising fifteen feet to ground level, striated with previous cienegas and plains like cross-section rings in a tree chronicling fifty thousand years of accumulated growth: making me realize that the whole planet is girdled by these rings, strata of soil built up since prehistory, and that the planet itself is the tree of life on which we grow.

March 30   Humm.

Sitting with the Mellors at the ranch house table talking about the thick-billed parrot which once migrated to the Huachuca Mountains. Speaking of the food that each habitat must provide for a creature to remain there, Cassie says, "Oh, that reminds me, I've let the six hummingbird feeders go empty. Would you refill them for me?" She had always allowed at least one feeder to be full of the red sweet liquid the hummingbirds had come to expect after so many years. The black-chinned and broad-billed hummingbirds returning from migration had buzzed the window to remind us of our duty. Taking the gallon jug of hummingbird food from the refrigerator and the twelve-foot aluminum ladder from behind the house, I came around to the window by the living room where the row of feeders pointed an empty accusing finger. A black-chinned, who was among the first to return, feeling he should be first to partake of the afternoon repast, sat on the broad lid to the jug as I climbed the ladder. Taking down the small inverted bottles from their wire hangers, I started to fill the first bottle as an iridescent broad-tail on his way up the Huachucas came closer to see exactly what was happening, then backed off a few inches as another came buzzing in to sip from the bottle still in my hand. And the word was out. From nests as delicate as spider webs the hummingbirds appeared as though out of nowhere while I poured from the great jar of Kool aid-like hummingbird goody. The black-chinned who had ridden up the ladder with me poking his head down into the wide-mouth gallon jug. And soon all about me dozens of hummingbirds spinning and whizzing like a planetarium of action; antimatter spinning through black holes in space and materializing again, coming up under my arm, across my ear onto my shoulder, my forearm, sitting on my head, buzzing, whirring, supersonic wings spinning in that unique rotary motion that allows their angular descent and amazing rises through space. I could no sooner fill one bottle and hang it up than hummers would be sitting on my fingers sipping, waiting for me to release the bottle so that they might drink more. One broad-bill perched incredibly on my nose, looking straight into my eyes like a fly pressed against a spaceship window. So much for us to see in each other's reality. The softest sensation I have ever experienced in nature: a hummingbird sitting on my forearm, whirring and sizzling, feeling like petals opening from a flower growing out of roots anchored in my nervous system, nerve ends fluttering out, indistinguishable from the sizzling hum of these tiny birds chattering that red delightful dessert was being served. Twelve feet up on the aluminum ladder surrounded by hummingbirds, my shoulders decorated with perched feathered epaulets, at my wrists hanging from the corner of my shirt fine iridescent cufflinks, tiny and full of life, like electrons whirring through molecular space seeking their haven. I felt like a nursing boar, my offspring two dozen whizzing hummers, my breasts those six jars filled with sugar and red food coloring, my nipples those long glass tubes reflected in the window before me. There could be nothing gentler or more violent than two hummingbirds mating, nothing more delicate or more like the collision of planets in space.

APRIL

April 1
April Fool's Day—
a species celebrates its involution.

SENT ACCEPTANCE TODAY to an invitation by the University of Syracuse to be guest poet for their Earth Week celebrations leading up to Environmental Teach-In Day on April 22. Thoughts of returning to the industralized Northeast from which I sprang. How to take a sense of sanctuary with me, internalized as the essence of planet stewardship, to the smokestack ironworks of the cities: to bring sanctuary to the 'quad', to displace political harangue with the poetry of organic revolution. To communicate the essence of revolution: to re-volute, to come back, to return to the source. To partake of change, to come out heads up, spine like the earth's axis, humming the melody of the sphere. How to communicate the pulsing re-volution which brings man back to his center, life and art made one through meditative recognition of the planet's life spirit. To invoke mindfulness as a celebration of stewardship, a survival technique to raise consciousness, to see the divine as it becomes all about us. The organic revolutionary stands within me comparing the two environments of the golden quietude of the sanctuary and the mumbling of the city—two states of mind mutually conscious of the synapse between them. Our outer resources, the planet's ancient mineral treasury, her dowry, depleted in direct proportion to the depletion of inner resources of modern man. The strip mining of the planet directly related to the strip-mined heart, the inner landscape decimated and devoid of respect. As man has moved farther from the heart's oasis toward the concrete breast of overcrowded cities he has fed those cities with the diminishing fossil blood of the planet. Burning dark anthracite corpuscles to turn the generators that light the night and make the streets safe for the internally injured. The stars go out one by one like the embers of an exhausted fire. We spend the dowry and plan divorce, seeking other planets for our bed.

How ironic that the University of Syracuse should offer me round-trip passage when fourteen years ago they turned down my student application noting that I didn't step to the Ivy League drummer, but if I could survive a year in any other 'acceptable' college they would allow me into the fold. Now having lived at sanctuary nine months, the period of gestation through which we all must pass, I return to their European campus to bring them back into the fold, to rejoin the Planet Family.

April 4   *Rudder-tailed grackles. An ancient*
              turkey vulture circles in return.

It's seven a.m. and already spring rises over the purple Huachucas. Mating songs everywhere: cinnamon, mauve, cream, ebony, ivory, bone, scarlet, gold and pollen yellow featherlings spiral and twist in the cienega mating dance. So many resettling after the cold winter, recongregating, socializing, meeting old friends and new mates, class reunion at sanctuary. Clear days with much sun. The raccoon visiting the tree by the porch. Tara simmering.

April 6   *The jays are back in force.*

Jays are the policemen of the woods. Here the Mexican jay and scrub jay patrol treetop and brushy swale castigating intruders. In their raucous investigations they lead us to the great horned owl who nests in the willow by the stream. Harassing him for nestlings picked from their perch at night, the jays announce for a mile around that public enemy number one has been discovered. Owl's great head pivots grumpily, attempting to avoid the necessity to move on as the jays' reconnaissance continues through the treetops and over the ridge. Ardent outlaws often make adept policemen. The jays account for the destruction of perhaps half of other birds' fallen nestlings, yet wail their angry innocence to the befuddled owl.

April 8   *Yellow-winged blackbirds. Asparagus at sanctuary.*

Once cultivated, now wild, 'volunteer' asparagus stalks rise to spring-chant harvesting. Of the hundred scattered ferns emerging, one out of ten is taken, the four inch spear clipped to regrow again within the week. A constancy of taking and replenishing. This asparagus once enslaved in long straight rows, irrigated, harvested, banded and sold, now escaped to sanctuary, surviving civilization to return to the wild.

All sorts of returning friends: the birds acknowledge the greeting of the gay Mimosa family, cactus bud opens to porcupine's indifferent inquiry, skunk and coatimundi sniff the javelina tracks, gazing at a pocket gopher in the field; great gray tree squirrels peer down on deer and yearling fawn. Cottonwoods greening toward the early sun of spring.

Part of my stewardship seems to be actuated in the writing I do each morning, to allow sanctuary to reach everywhere. So much to do through this Gutenberg gene which seems to find the heart's energy manifest as language shared like a healing chant or a prayer book for the benefit of the whole. We steward the mother sphere in every way possible; we do the best we can any way we can. 'To walk in a sacred manner', as was the American Indian way: to make an art of life.

April 10   *A reunion with friends and returning warblers.*

Patricia's friend since kindergarten, Patrick Silva, arrives with suitcase and cookbook in hand to familiarize himself with the sanctuary so as to steward the land while we are on the East Coast. His blue eyes a crystalline reflection of the Southwestern sky. Coming from Bolinas, California, to spend a week with us before we depart, cooking his epicurean wonders to our delighted palate: soufflés and quiche, fresh asparagus hollandaise, chutney and mango goodies. How lovely to have a fine cook, organic revolutionary, old friend partaking of the sanctuary family, to awake to huevos rancheros on the morning porch. Patrick's quietude coming and going as peaceful as verse from Gibran, a quiet smile born of years of living alone amid the tribe, finding himself in quiet turnings in his candlelit cabin above the crashing Pacific.

April 13

Before leaving the sanctuary to Patrick and the Indian spirits I go down to the cattailed spring to welcome the first red-winged blackbird returned for spring, and to perform the first of the ceremonies which over these next two weeks will unite me with my fellow beings and the land. The first wedding is begun wading knee deep into the dark waters to gently snip the maturing cattails from their long green stems. A fine yellow pollen dusts the base of each shaken cattail as I carefully carry four mature cattail heads to the bank under the shade of the mulberry tree. The yellow pollen alive upon my hand, its complete history coded in each grain floating toward the cienega to further propagate its kind.

Following an ancient ritual learned from a local Apache farmer we begin the prayer for life. A fifteen square foot area is designated as the 'holy ground', four crosses placed north, south, east and west to designate the cardinal points of each creature's inner compass. Shaking the pollen toward the cross to the north I repeat,

"When the earth was first created—
when the sky was first created—
in the beginning, when all was started
in the center of the earth—
God's sacred pollen—
a cross of sacred pollen—"

turning to the east to shake the golden pollen on the
cross of dry mesquite I repeat,

"living sacred pollen—
a cross of sacred pollen
breathing in four directions—
God's cross of sacred pollen—"

to the south, dispersing the pollen from the third cattail I repeat,

"my own, my sacred pollen—
my own, my prayer—
like four rays, power is flowing forth
from the tips of my fingers—
now it is known that I go forth with power—"

to the west, where the sun disappears like life which
goes on elsewhere, I repeat,

"on the surface of the world
sad things are occurring, bad things are
    occurring,
sickness and evil are occurring,
wrong knowledge is occurring—
in four directions these things are dispersed
    and fade away—
God comes to live with man—

the breath of God—
God's sacred pollen—
God himself
living sacred pollen."

There is a quietude after this short ceremony in which all the creatures of sanctuary seem hushed. The redwing modestly accepts what appears to him a simple homecoming greeting. There is nothing foreign in this ceremony, a ritual of man celebrating and reaffirming life. To find the Apache and the homesteader within each of us. To be free of partial ways of seeing. To come to the surface, man alive, rejoicing in his living. Pollen on my palms and hands, I am impregnated with the earth and carry sanctuary like an embryo within to the life-seekers of the crowded city cave.

April 14   *The orioles arrive as we depart.*

Preparations complete, suitcases packed, the necessary books and the ear-worn manuscript of our sanctuary accumulation readied for the great jump across the continent. Sanctuary established in each cell to be invoked at the proper moment for a proper wedding with the land on this first nationally recognized holy week, culminating in complete respect for the Mother, on Earth Day.

April 15   *Heading east, colliding with the sun,*
                    toward Earth Day benediction.

Over the intercom the pilot tells us that the anti-gravitational device in which we are being transported consumes twelve thousand pounds of fuel per hour. Fifty thousand pounds of fuel, eighty-five hundred gallons, one mile each four and one-half seconds. What part of me, acculturated or deconditioned participates in this great exhalation of toxins into the communal air, for the sake of the soft green planet below?

April 16   *Arrive Syracuse as the elf owl arrives at sanctuary.*

Met at the airport by the old friend who arranged this earth-invocation on the campus of the University. As I bend to pick up my suitcase the turquoise and silver Santa Domingo healing necklace which Patricia placed around my neck in the Tucson airport breaks and scatters the Southwest across terrazzo floor of the American Airlines reception lounge.

Syracuse is an industrial backwash, its city seal three belching smokestacks. But the land about is somehow still able to receive spring, though forty year old potato farms, soil dead as styrofoam, are fertilized each year to replace some of what has been removed in the continual enslavement of land now only a cushion for roots, no longer fertile. Huge mechanical spreaders broadcast white powder across the stiff soil, cosmetics on a corpse. Yet even here a crocus or wild iris emerges where the tractor has passed.

193

Poetry of the life quest begun after the audience joins with me pronouncing the 'Humm' to be heard arising from the earth in quiet arroyos or by a softly whispering stream in the wilderness. The high adventure of the wilderness brought indoors. Joined with the audience, seeing with them from another mountain the valley I have just left. The sacred seed of earth as rice passed in straw basket, rained by each so very gently on his neighbor, passing straw vessel like an ethereal spirit from one to the other: the hostile exorcising themselves, the gentle absorbing it and bathing each other in glistening grain. Much joy and some slight rebirth as I move through the colorful incarnations of the students gathered to partake of this spring incantation. Poems of sanctuary accompanied by colored slides projected behind me on the glass bead screen. Pollen floating over the audience shaken from the cattails collected by the students and brought to this earth offering, the assemblage like an oasis in the red brick colonial desert of the University.

April 18   *Second invocation and more.*

Three long poems read to flute and guitar, cello and viola, the audience of one eye bathed in the colors reflected from the screen. The audience of one breath, breathing with each line, all of us walking together by the stream, sharing the kingbird burial. Many have returned from last night's celebration bringing loved ones and cattails to continue the growth of the collective evolutionary force projected from our congregation. Scores of people hands joined, their cells bonded each to the other like molecules entwined in a strand of DNA, our mutual purpose the integration of all life. While so many of the audience were attentive to the celebration, a few in the back of the auditorium sipped beer and appraised women like meat dangling in a butcher's window, to which a friend whispered, "If you offer words of the spirit to a man who does not ask for them, you waste the words. But if a man asks for those words and you do not offer them, you waste the man." After the reading the majority sat quietly, wedded in silence, touched by sanctuary.

April 20   *East along the Mohawk to*
                              family reunion.

In homeground Albany visiting with my parents, brother and wife arriving for the first reunion in several years, all our families together: my mother and father, my brother and his wife and daughter, myself, Patricia and Tara celebrating the family clan together. The whole human family incarnate in our ancient familial gestures.

April 21

About to head to New York City to participate in the Union Square planet-conscious poetry readings when it occurs to me that there is in Albany a new division of the State University of New York built over a field I played in as a child, where hardwood forests, birched, birded and deered, have been replaced by the Rockefeller Coliseum architecture of wasted materials and enslaved planet, covered over by the concrete incantations of man's fear of himself taken to the second power—a fear of nature, a distrust of forces by which he has been created.

A call to the University reveals interest in an Earth Day reading; I am invited to come that evening to speak to an ecology workshop. The class continues an hour as I propose a study of Land Stewardship, an in-depth interlocking of our mind with the gentle mind of the planet. Attempting to instill a further involvement in the home on which we ride; planet stewards, citizens of Aquarian World Village. Whole Earth Sanctuary.

April 22   *Earth Day.*

Reading poetry of sanctuary and its effect on our particular reality, in a great stone room replacing the meadow I ran in years ago as a young bush warrior, rabbits scurrying from my stick. The movements of the heart cadenced in the audience to the rise and fall of these words, translated from the mindstuff to the overtones of language. We had all written the poems I am reading, the Collective Cortex chiming unanimous among the cross-legged tribe seated with me on the floor. Yearling Tara saunters up into my lap while I

196

am reading, a coquette if ever I saw one, a blessing in mystical mudraforms from her tiny gyrating fingers, her palm outward to the assembled group in the Fear Not gesture. Great warmth from the hundred or so listeners, another mystical union with the land.

April 23   *Revisiting hardschool NYC*
                    looking for friends' faces,
                    a day of déjà vu—
                    everybody looks familiar
                    but I can't recall anyone's name.

Hiking through the cliffs, canyons and outcroppings of the mineral environment of the city. An ecology of extremes: fragile/powerful man, presently the leading edge of evolution, enclosed in the mineral world's mastodon-like solidity. Surrounded by an ecosystem of his own making: potted tropical plants thrive in steam-heated living rooms, fuchsias suspended from the sills; the flora and fauna of introduced wildlings abound. Dogs from the tundra and veldt, cats from the Sudan, pigeons (the European rock dove), English house sparrows, starlings, the brown and black rats, mythical alligators in the sewers; species out of their native environment like man himself.

In the human ecosystem of the city, the intense overcrowding necessitates that one does not push away those one comes in contact with. The pushing causes waves in the pool of humanity which make all uncomfortable; instead we must embrace, leaving room for all, each more comfortable within.

Walking the city streets I see all the species of the Animal Kingdom reenacted in the faces about me. Park Avenue swans and matronly elk. Mustachioed weasels. Bull-faced commuters. Young raccoon toughs congregate on a street corner admiring lunch-boxed construction bears, eyeing prancing teenage deer. Bearded wildebeests. A sleek Fifth Avenue quail sharing a cab with an African crested bird of paradise. A high nasal Long Island bushtit. Hitch-hiking backpacked wood ducks extend a primary hoping to catch a ride down the Atlantic flyway. Trash picker opossums recycle the litter of life. Shuffling badgers. All the creatures are here having taken human form to complete their animal destiny.

April 24

Walking gray Third Avenue
thinking of green sanctuary,
wondering as I cross to the Bowery
how living in the city
man might find his vision—
    hearts meeting along a stream
    brown eyes peering into mine
    all life beating in our chest
    a harmonic struck
    between life forms.

Then a bowery exile stumbles
and falls like a wounded deer
spastic legs kicking

from ragged trousers
unable to rise
a dull rush of violet
in thick matted hair.
Recognizing myself in another
beside cobblestone river—
cars rushing by
bloated metallic salmon
running upstream
against the flow
on their way to propagation
and death.

And I discover again
that even in the city
all life breathes—
the Earth sighs and murmurs
in the sun.

April 25   *Return to sanctuary.*

In airplane time machine heading away from city
back toward the green eye of God I replay the mind's
tape of the experiences we have just undergone; the
often unsuccessful overcrowded experiment of New
York City. When the density of animal populatións increases to a point of stress, an epidemic often occurs to
prune the population to a size supportable by the habitat. In wild animals it is often called rabies, in man it is
called war. But man is capable of guiding himself, of
controlling population growth without battle or plague.

199

And we come home to sanctuary, further evolved. Bliss unfurling like the green leaf-fans of cottonwoods. Squirrels seeking squirrels in acrobatic pyrotechnics, the Olympics of the mating season. House finches singing territory to their mates. Phoebes beneath the eaves. Raccoon's amber eyes aging to the yelp of joyous dogs. What an erotic dance spring is! How healthy this planet mind that clocks the return of growth and further life. Now we are even more wedded to the land after the incantations in Albany homeland past. All life is one: simply life, a manifestation of molecular deities dancing at the center of each cell; life, how fantastic!

One of these days I'll give up the alphabet and return to pictographs; my handwriting is almost pictographic anyhow.

April 26   *And on the eleventh day he rested.*

Last night Patricia woke itching, hives across her abdomen, back and shoulders. An allergic reaction, the toxins of the city coming like slag to the surface. This morning a noticeable tremble in the hands. We are reorienting now to the natural rhythms of the land. The predominance of lateral metallic motion, the constant flow of automobiles, buses and trucks through the city, cutting the measurable electromagnetic field of the planet at a ninety degree angle, creates a classic example of a generator—the urban generator having its own frequency, one not necessarily in tune with the natural frequency of those who live within its vibratory field. Large cities produce an unnatural modulation inharmonic with the human body, tuned through evolution to the planet, which makes it difficult to stay centered. If the rhythm of the individual becomes that of the dynamo of the city, he will literally go out of his mind, technological compression distorting the inherent melody of his substance. So it becomes necessary to rebalance, as did the Pueblo Indian listening for the beat of his heart to come into cadence with the beat of the Earth Mother, to come into tune with the natural melody of the sphere.

Slowly our nerves readjust, spring coming once again to the mind's continuum. A phoebe sings territorial defeat just above the room in which I write. How well our brother creatures comprehend the ongoing glow and spark of things—this defeated bird sailing from the tree in search of open territory, the victor also singing, a chorus of the rise and fall of the life flow, each out to find himself in another, seeking his kind in color and airdance, singing. Spring.

If we could impart only one thought to every being in the world, it would be that there is no such thing as weeds. On every level this is so, with people no less than plants.

What peace can come from technological change, what pearl rises from the speck in the oyster's eye!

MAY

May 1
May Day at the center.
Wildlings all about.

T HE LAST SUMMER RESIDENTS arrive, whitewing
and kingbird, the two species we have tended,
one healed, one buried.

At the southerly end of the cienega, near where willows flare to border the marsh, a small ancient wooden
shack where wire and fence tools were once stored
leans against the wind. In the corner of the shack a
tumble of sticks, eighty year old copper-plate barbed
wire, feathers, stones, dried leaves, the packrats' great
homestead: a century-old tumble of willow and currant, woven with dried orchids of a dozen years, faded
buttercups, primrose and blue-eyed grass intertwine in
the massive chaos of random yarrow. The patinaed
cartridges of dead cowboys hidden in its midst like
kidney stones; coins; the missing eyepiece of Mr. Haro,
long since gone seeking Apaches toward Freeman
Spring, never returning. In this archive tended by the
packrats who come to survey the house is the history
of the land, the pollen and seeds of plants long since
climaxed and past.

From a passageway beneath the castle big ears then
long whiskers then a squirrel-sized fawn-colored body
emerges followed by a long furry tail. Sensing humans
watching he retreats, not as fond of man as his common
black and brown rat cousins who followed *Homo sapi-
ens* around the world from central Asia. About the
passageway seeds, nuts and green plant matter litter the

splintered wooden floor. A choice wrinkled apple, an added delight to sustain his short life, waits as he awaits the appetite of so many others. A staple in the diet of foxes, coyotes, bobcats, horned owls, hawks and snakes, his life expectancy is short, two or three years at the most. He is host for triatoma, the kissing bug, whose bite in the tropics causes Chagas disease, yet is undisturbed by the parasite's presence, considerably more wary of the golden eyes that seek him out for food. And it is supposed that Darwin contracted Chagas disease in his historic voyage; later confined to his study where with tremendous effort, yet accepting this further manifestation of evolution, he formulated his vision of the life progression.

Is Fyodor the sophisticated cousin of these country field dwellers? Protected in the walls and under the roof of our homestead he might live ten years, feeding on the fruits of our labors, collecting at will my pens and pencils and any small change left to tempt his fascination for shiny objects. Fyodor acquires our trinkets as memorabilia for his time capsule to remain long after we have both passed on.

May 2

Spring rises from earth to sky. The lives of minerals glisten like iridescent beetles fossilized by the sun. The green lives of trees, shrubs, cacti, flowers, lengthen toward grandfather sun. Willows stretch and yawn. Birds claim territory and nest, songchant lifting toward mountain horizon softened by the warm breeze. Rac-

205

coon and deer peer brown-eyed from a green thicket. The horses and dogs shed their winter compensations. Snow gone from the high Huachucas, and we return like spring a single note in the melody.

May 3   *Earth warms mineral memory.*

In the molecular pulsing of minerals lies the subtle essence of life: an opportunity to see life in its slightest measurable incarnation. Are minerals unthinking, without memory? How long does a stone stay warm after it has been removed from the sun's heat? What is memory? It has been conjectured that if another life form were to be discovered it would in all probability be a crystal.

May 4   *Vivekananda and I,*
                         some poems
                         and a sleeping bag
                         gone for a ride
                         to think, reorient
                         to time and space . . .

Duster and I descending through desert grasslands meet Apaches and roadrunners along the way. Scattering a flock of browsing monks—brown-hooded black-bodied cowbirds heading for a purple flowering ocatillo, disappearing like a swarm of bees. Onto the saguaro-forested desert floor past a rattlesnake too lazy to coil in defiance of the tremors Duster's thousand pounds send through the hard baked earth. The white and yellow lotus blossoms of the saguaro trumpet the high spring desert sun. Purple-red ocatillo blossoms climbing long witch-fingered stalks. A yellow little leaf palo verde shades our restings and our lunch shared with jays and thrashers. Spring desert blooming. Last year's rains feeding a dozen humming colors, nectar everywhere.

May 5   *Cinco de Mayo, Latin Independence*
         Day in Tucson. The ROTC building
         occupied with the anguish of the deaths
         at Kent State.

Blue-eyed grass and daisy forms flowing like a robe along either side of the cienega.

May 6   *Wild asparagus by the stream—a green*
         breakfast.

Overhead a western tanager in the quince conversing with an olivaceous flycatcher. Above us a pair of sun-opaqued red-tailed hawks soar on gilded primaries, translucent edge upon the rising thermals.

In the evening I water pyracantha planted by the house to attract the birds which get drunk on its berries. A dead mountain king snake wound about its shadowy base—sinuous river toward the void, forgotten ribs holding forgotten body—returning, feeding the planet which feeds all.

*May 7   Duster to foal in five weeks, looks like she
          swallowed a baby grand.*

Patty and Tara bubbling with earth joy.
Indian spirits chase the mindstuff like wind filling a
soaring kite. Mockingbirds return, each an old friend
mimicking a universe of fellow species.

*May 8   Morning with the four year old
                          Indian girl buried by the
                          adobe ruins south of the house.*

The Indian spirits so prevalent on this land permeate
us. Sometimes I sense my feet rooted invisibly in the
earth; when I lift them, the magnetic draw continues
up to my shoulders. I feel as though I've just laid my
hunting spear aside nearby and am waiting for the
Spirit to direct me toward the silent forest. I am somewhere between observation and prayer.
    It nears the end of our year in sanctuary and our
lives expand toward the tribal homeground of northern
California—old friends missed, company for Tara's
growing intuitions, Patricia humming that fertile song.
I suspect our son is on his way; we'll meet him in California no doubt.

May 10   Winds prune ancient willows.

Sky clear except for a few puffed spring clouds;
one sees in all directions a distant mountain horizon.
We are floating in a dish of universe—life in a living

amphitheater.

May 11

Five acrobatic acorn woodpeckers in an oak tangle. Sunset javelina descend the hill toward evening waters, nostrils flaring between blunt tusks, sensing my watching, steel gray bristles against the rusting shafts of grama.

May 12　　　*Bullock's orioles arrive, Wilson's warblers depart after a week-long stopover in migration.*
Hooded orioles squabble territory.

To Ramsey Canyon, carved into the eastern slope of the Huachucas, to see Carrol Peabody, broad-backed twinkling-eyed foreman for the dam, at his Mile-Hi 'hummingbird capital of the USA' to stay the night and watch the myriad hummingbird rainbows at the feeders; his wife Joan able to identify each species by the hum of its wings. Then up the box canyon following the stream through maples, oaks, pine, juniper, Spanish bayonet, yucca and our favorite tree, the great peeling-barked sycamore reminiscent of our California madrone forest companions. In the brush of the canyon slopes the song of the coppery-tailed trogon, a visitor from South America much sought by the bird watchers on the path, their heads cocked like ravens. And on up into the canyon to soak hot feet in the waters gushing

forth from the sheer stone cliffs which abruptly end
the path.

May 14   *Red-winged blackbird, western kingbird*
              intersong undulating in the oaks,
              heads thrown back, trumpet chimes.
              Pronghorn grazing by green arroyo scar.

A white-tailed doe saunters down deerpath hill a
few yards from the house on her way to the cienega.
Across muddy sedge-bottom to green swatches beneath
apple trees—standing on hindlegs to reach the dark
tasty apples of last autumn, browsing through mid-
morning.

May 15   *Even a disturbed area can be calming.*

Tiny orange-blossomed mallow, thistle poppy and
calabash squash flowering where trucks have gouged
the earth.

May 16   *Temperatures in mid-nineties.*

Work begun to complete the dam now that the rains
have abated. Wingwalls raised, backhoe planet dentistry once again trenching mother earth 'for her own
good.' A delicate balance of stewardship with, rather
than over, the earth.

May 17   *Jimson cornucopia along arroyo bottom.*
           Sacred and powerful datura awaiting
           experienced hands. Mescalito chanting
           in the underbrush.

At twilight three great blue heron loping above the tree-topped stream, settling atop tallest cottonwood, long serpentine necks rising as from Pharaoh's crown, their six foot wingspan folded neatly about a blue-gray body.

May 18   *Buttercups and daisies. More dam*
           hassles.

Backhoe tipped by five tons of rock slid from a truck, upsetting Newton like a teacup.

May 19   *Vesak full moon. Buddha's birthday.*

Riding with friends through mountain trails that lead into the San Rafael Valley, ducking manzanita and mesquite, we approach a drying water hole too closely, the horses' legs sinking into deep mud around the stagnant pond. Rearing like dinosaurs caught in a prehistoric ooze, the horses' genetic panic tosses us from the saddle into the rich mire of the receding water hole. We three approach a nearby rancher's home leading our horses, the mud caked and dried upon us, three Neanderthals and our captured beasts approaching civilization out of the primal ooze. Greeted by a compassionate chuckle, a hot toddy and a warm bath.

May 20

A couple of coyote pups, mother shot or poisoned by state decree, run the ridge behind the house. The dogs join them for breakfast then trot home again exhausted. Over the hills the coyote pups wail and yelp in their lost play, heading away from sanctuary toward poison lures on the rolling grasslands. Sodium fluoroacetate, the infamous poison 1080, injected into donkey carcasses distributed on the open range in the guise of aid to the cattle industry by governmental wildlife services. These poison carcasses spread throughout the countryside to kill the myth of the killer coyote. 1080 works slowly and agonizingly on the central nervous system of a coyote, causing cramps and vomiting as he panics and begins to run in sheer terror until at last he collapses and dies in kicking convulsions. Ironically what occurs is not the death of a bloodthirsty creature but the decimation of an important natural predator. It is thought by some that when the coyotes are killed at the cattleman's request or the state's whim the rabbit population increases and the grasses which the cattlemen depend on for feed are chewed to stump by the burgeoning rabbit tribes. Also in the irony of unlacing the fine workings of the net of nature comes the problem rather than the solution: the normal behavior of the resident coyote (which does not include, as some fantasize, the tearing of birthing calves from the womb of the cow) is altered within an outlaw population of

212

coyotes who may indeed not stay on the poisoned open range but run in gangs across private grasslands, marauding as they go. The poisons creating the problem they are intended to solve.

Cattlemen kill coyotes in a throwback to the frontier consciousness where all wildlife was considered as 'varmints', threats to civilization and Christianity. I once saw a letter written by an official of a state fish and game agency which said that guarding livestock from wildlife predation was a Christian duty having its roots in the Bible, man being the dominant shepherd over all forms of life. This was a predominant motivation of many of the early pioneers who considered the natural earth as a symbol of Satan: the wilderness something to be subdued; man's Christian duty to burn and cut the forest and grassland, to destroy wildlife as a test that God had put man here to meet. When you chopped down a tree or cleared the land you were doing God's work. When you shot a mountain lion or a wolf or poisoned a coyote you were putting Satan back in his place.

Two coyotes, frightened and lost, pursue their God-given directive to exist, passing fence posts which like civilization elude grace with a glance in either direction. Two soft pups following a ravine past the carcass of a poisoned coyote which in its turn, eaten by golden eagle, ringtail and fox, furthers the deluge and the blight of man's deadly unconsciousness. Two coyotes lost beyond sanctuary.

May 21   *This arises, that becomes.*

New grass appears above the dried stalks of the old. The birds have returned and mated, their nests like tiny wombs everywhere about the sanctuary. Never have we been so aware of life. All about us spring has turned plant to flower as flower becomes seed of new births. Our hands against Duster's underbelly feel the stubborn kicking of the colt. Red-winged blackbird just fledged from the nest wobbles in first flight. Tiny frogs called peepers hereabouts chirp to the sun mellowing on the western horizon. Turkey vultures spread in the crimson sunset sky.

May 22

Gardening in the vegie patch thinking of Azul's son's birth at Table Mountain Ranch last week. Awaiting the birth of Duster's foal and their ability to travel to the Pacific. The letter from Azul and Ishtar describing the experience in the hand-built redwood pyramid on the plateau slope overlooking the Albion River rushing to join the ocean three miles to the west. Through an open door a sparrow rises high into the cupola rafters to peer down quizzically at Azul and Ishtar practicing for the delivery with an antique wooden doll. The sparrow breaking into song as their son's placental ocean bursts from Ishtar's cave. A new world coming forth below the sparrow's lilting birthchant. The cervix stretched to allow heaven to pass. Three hummingbirds press against the rough mullioned window, noisy relatives attempting to outdo each other in naming the new family member. "Fern beauty," sizzles one. "Lizard wing?" whizzes another. "Lightning," buzzes the third. And at that moment Vajra crowns to a Tibetan chant, named for the vajra-lightning which permeates the harmonious being, coming forth to join the Planet Family. An ecstatic sparrow in the rafters, swallows chattering in their pews beneath the eaves, hummers gossiping at the windows, a condor spiraling slowly upward welcoming the birth of the generation which must save him from extinction—a generation of stewards born in the midst of the world.

Dear one on this natural birth
all feet touch our mother earth
all hands coming together in a ring of fire
welding us each to the other.
Each breath so perfect
plowed pulsing through the blood
a unison beyond the body
each breath breathing with the deep
breath of the mountain
the heart coming into the Greater Heart.

May 23   *Our son conceived at midnight on*
                  Patricia's twenty-sixth birthday.

Born to human form, the mark of grace. And may the body into which the spirit is poured be sufficient to fulfill its karma. Noah, named for the first planet steward, enters Patricia's body, come to recreate paradise. We are reborn with the birth of each child. And how could it have been otherwise? So right and well drawn from the molecules of our genetic dust.

May 27   *Four kingbirds hatched in the nest beside the corral. Sparrows in the adobe wall. Primrose, nightshade.*

May 31   *That which is unloved decomposes quickly.*

Stewardship is rooted in the recognition that the land reflects the consciousness living upon her. Native peoples striving to live in harmony with their environment honored that which supported them, often let pass the first or second individual of the species they were collecting or hunting, eluding the seeded and the pregnant. They maintained a balance which fed and clothed them, which housed and gave spirit to their life. The conquistador and the cowboy seeing the open grasslands of the Southwest made no attempt to cover their tracks. Where the white man camped the ground was left scarred, where he farmed the soil was robbed and discarded, where he ranched the earth was gouged and stripped. Life became a commodity and the possibilities for a 'quick killing' were cast like poker chips on the table. When the earth is not respected it erodes, when the integrity of the grass is not considered it diminishes, when the wildlife and the streams become expendable they retreat into extinction and grace is destroyed. The earth moans and dries, supporting less life, offering less harmony. The land requires the re-

216

spectful attention of those who would see this earth garden whole again, restored. Stewardship is a recognition of responsibilities, an honoring of the gifts of the sweet earth.

JUNE

June 1
Planet mind rising.
Wind's song, heart's home.

T HERE IS A NEW CONSCIOUSNESS rising from a generation of planet-conscious beings. Though many lament the passing of so much of our wilderness environment, too many miss the point. We indeed are not the most deprived men ever to have lived, unlucky and haunted. We are instead the luckiest of men, for at no other time in his history has man had the opportunity to be so sensitized to nature. The passing of the Merriam elk and the grizzly bear, the passenger pigeon and the buffalo, the thick-billed parrot and the imperial ivory-billed woodpecker, only brings us closer to the source from which we each sprang. We live in a time punctuated by the well-noted cries of vanishing species, yet never so greatly has our imagination been stimulated by the circling of an eagle or the tracks of a mountain lion. The creatures past are a sacrifice for our greater involvement in the planet and all that lives upon her. It is not that we live in the best of all possible worlds, but that we are sensitized to the best possibilities of our world.

Those who serve the planet know there is no buying or selling nor ownership of the land, recognize that we are as transient as the birds; and though we sing out territory in the windblown hum of barbed wire, the planet belongs to time, to evolution.

Hoeing the earth to plant living seeds, humming Vajra's birth to an inquisitive bunting iridescent on a nearby thistle poppy. The dogs arrive one by one, clumps of porcupine quills like reeds growing from the tips of their noses. I sit on the porch patiently clipping and pulling the quills as the three dogs take their turn stoically, White Guy dejected as a muddy child scrubbed behind the ears. Returning to the garden thinking of the rediscovery of life which is birth, the muscles stretched then relaxed once again, the channel past, the joyous continuum as clear as the porcupined nose on our face. And we are all writing the same poem under the same heaven and who would have imagined the essence of mind to be intrinsically pure: the real pure land, the pure real land.

June 3   *The vision of the quest is the quest itself.*

There is no goal but doing. The vision revealed by this year at sanctuary is that the quest is the path, as stewardship is a road one travels not a place one is going. The song has come to guide the ongoing journey. And the song tells me to trust my vision and pray that we are blessed.

June 4   *Cienega discourse.*

Cicadas buzz with solar energy. Crickets and fireflies measure the evening. At night the frogs converse: Hrepot hrepot? Ziggy ziggy!

June 5   *Fyodor drops a friend by for breakfast.*

Awoke this morning the left side of my face swollen so that I cannot open my eye—'kissed' by triatoma twice on the cheek during the night. His relationship to Fyodor not to my greatest liking, but that is a part of stewardship. Better to be bitten by a mosquito or a triatoma than to live in the crushing noise and biting smog of the city. We have found it easier to entrust a child to the rhythms of nature than to the perpetual motion of technology. We would rather have our child wander in a field with the possibility of a slightly toxic meeting with some remarkable and frightened wildling than to allow that child the city street or an abandoned icebox or unguarded swimming pool. We have a better chance of surviving within nature than without it.

June 6   *Tenth of an inch of rain, Phainopeplia bathing in an oak cathedral.*

June 7

If it were not for man's technological failures in the past, his inability to mechanically overcome nature, the balance would probably have been upset long ago, but it is nature's intricate and ongoing evolution which has allowed the land to heal most wounds in time. Let us praise crabgrass as a manifestation of the ability of nature to maintain over all attempts at cultivation. Crabgrass is a sign that nature still exists.

June 8   *The dam complete.*

The cienega is saved and sighs in warm dark mud. A unique species of planetdom surviving to tell the tale of how it was, and how it can be if only we care.

June 9

First it was the mockingbird who initiated us, then left us on our own. Next the Cassin's kingbird, dead in my palm. Then Charlie One Wing, healed a bit lopsided, freed before dove season, a side swing to the south. Like a flashback another mockingbird dazed in the tall grama in need of a twenty-four hour rest stop. Then for months in the playpen in our bedroom the horned lark which we have now brought to the Arizona Sonora Desert Museum to live out its earth bound days in a near natural environment. We say good-bye to Horny and head back to sanctuary, stopping to have Divine Providence lubed at the crossroads.

We live in a world regulated
        by Natural Law.
What goes up

comes down.
For each force
    comes another.
And that's the way it is—
Anything else is an invention
    that things are otherwise
and we suffer the distortion.

The planet, like the mind,
responds to loving kindness
    in like manner.
We get what we give.

We live now
And now is when we must act wisely.

June 11   *A feast of grasshoppers.*

The grasshoppers are everywhere, enameled jewelry, red, green, blue, yellow, large as cicadas, animated brooches slaloming through the grasslands. Bear, raccoon, skunk, coatimundi, owl, flycatcher, hawk, snake make feast of the colorful delicacy that abounds in the grass forest jumping from orange-lichened rock to pale soil. The grasshopper tribes angle down the course of ravines past the magical deep-throated Jimson and the quiet deer. Grasshoppers everywhere like vitamins on the breakfast table, a supplement offered the creatures at sanctuary. Because of last year's wet winter the grasshopper population affords bountiful hors d'oeuvres in the short grass banquet.

June 12   *Nature's crop arising.*

Kingbirds out of nest learning flight to mother's piping.

June 14

Kingbirds gaining solo hours. Red-winged blackbird mother's swamp trill yodel to two fledglings swooping across the cienega.

June 15   *A wandering monk arrives.*

Japanese planet wanderer and poet monk Nanao comes to stay for our last days at sanctuary. Talk of caves and the lions and monks which inhabit them, creatures seeking a bit of shade. Nanao's friend Nancy returns to Tucson, a nurse of the first order, a Zen nun, requested by the family to continue tending Joseph Wood Krutch during the final course of his long illness.

June 16   *Chanting each evening the sun,*
                             Prajna Paramita.

Nanao and I climb the mesa to sit beneath the single oak which punctuates the open-topped plain, chanting down the sun with a Buddhist sutra. As the sun bursts like a grape on the planet rim, I mention to Nanao that before it gets dark he might like to see the far end of the stream where it disappears underground, and then walk the mile back to sanctuary. We head north across the mesa to take a shortcut, descending through ravines and arroyos, over another hill and around an unfamiliar outcropping. The sun nearly drained, the sky a scarlet flood. Dodging mesquite and century plant we climb down to the valley floor where we expect to find the creek—but we have lost our way, taking an easterly arroyo whose turns confuse us. And I say to him, hoping not to frighten him unduly, perhaps it will take a bit longer to find our way back. Nanao turns to me and smiles, "Oh, how can one get lost, it is such a small planet." And in a few minutes we are at the stream following the flow home.

June 18   *Nancy returns at sunset.*

In our year at sanctuary we have had the opportunity to speak with Dr Krutch only once, our conversation about animal communications a glowing directive from a man of considerable knowledge and sensitivity, though his illness could be felt across the room. Having brought clear energies to his final moments, Nancy tells us that Dr Krutch has finished his journey: a planet steward who gave himself to his vision of man's more complete return to the Planet Family in writings which began forty years ago, soon after the last passenger pigeon. With Dr Krutch's passing a year at sanctuary is nearly complete, and we somehow pass on with him.

June 20   *One departs so another may arrive.*

Duster foals at midnight, a sorrel colt with a white crescent blaze on his forehead giving him the name Half Moon, born during that season of the sky. Tara astride reclining colt, each nuzzling the other.

June 21, 1970   *Sun cycle, summer solstice.*

So many visions seen and recorded, so much absorbed and imprinted in the true art of living. The vision quest fulfilled. Life chiming like Genesis at the center of each cell. My heart an emerald like the cienega heart of the sanctuary. And we prepare to leave sanctuary with sanctuary within—placenta oasis, Noah suspended in the arc of Patricia's body. Noah returned, come to save his beloved animals. As his grandmother said the day he was born, "Noah was the only one God trusted."

East for Earth Day we had taken sanctuary with us like a meditation, the stewardship internalized, more an attitude than a discipline, deeply rooted in our human clay. Now Patricia has taken the seed within, aligning chromosomes as the original Noah matched pairs, brought two by two into that first sanctuary. And now Noah floats in Patricia's ocean, the ark builder come to preserve paradise.

Trust your vision
make it whole
    hold it like the Navajo
    his solemn desert oracle
    in quest of shaman passage
    gaining his healing chant
    guiding him through life.
Hold the vision
    constantly rising
    it is the way nature works
      through you
    it is the only self
      an everchanging underdream
    a vision (if you see it)
      up to you
    to make real.
Act on your vision
    and pray that you are blessed.

ABOUT THE AUTHOR

Stephen Levine, poet, editor and spiritual ecologist was born in the hardwood forests of upstate New York in 1937. He has previously published six books of poetry and prose and edited various publications, including the San Francisco Oracle. His work has been singled out for acclaim by Library Journal, Place magazine and the San Francisco Chronicle. He presently resides in the mammalian foothills of the Santa Cruz mountains overlooking the Pacific Ocean.

ABOUT THE ILLUSTRATOR

Armando Busick, an award-winning artist, art director for the Spiritual Community Guide, is well-known for his work which has been the focal point for dozens of fine book covers. He and Levine have worked together over the past eight years on numerous projects, including the San Francisco Oracle and Busick's PAGES FROM A TREE (Unity Press 1972).

This first edition of 5000 copies was printed on Georgia-Pacific Loyola Vellum and bound into a Beckett Cambric Cover; 1000 copies were clothbound. Postcards were printed on French Parchtone. The typeface used in the text is Continental with headlining in Trump Mediæval set by ATS of Mountain View on a Harris Fototronic System. Printed by offset lithography by Globe Printing Company of San Jose.

July at Sanctuary. From the book *Planet Steward:*
Journal of a Wildlife Sanctuary published by Unity Press.

August at Sanctuary. From the book *Planet Steward:*
Journal of a Wildlife Sanctuary published by Unity Press.

Trust your vision
make it whole
    hold it like the Navajo
    his solemn desert oracle
    in quest of shaman passage
    gaining his healing chant
    guiding him through life.

Hold the vision
    constantly rising
    it is the way nature works
        through you
    it is the only self
        an everchanging underdream
    a vision (if you see it)
        up to you
        to make real.
Act on your vision
    and pray that you are blessed.

December at Sanctuary. From the book *Planet Steward: Journal of a Wildlife Sanctuary* published by Unity Press.

Trust Your Vision. From the book *Planet Steward: Journal of a Wildlife Sanctuary* published by Unity Press.